BECOMING

RICH

Genevieve Davis

Becoming Rich

A Method for Manifesting Exceptional Wealth

GENEVIEVE DAVIS

CONTENTS

INTRODUCTION

Why listen to me?

1 This Book is for You

Mine is a true rags to riches experience.

Only a few years ago I lived in a tiny flat, working twelve hours a day in a factory for minimum wage. I was over £30,000 ($45,000) in credit card debt and had a £2600 ($4000) overdraft. I was moderately educated but unskilled and had few prospects for changing my situation in any conventional way. I sometimes wrote cheques for groceries I knew would bounce just so that I could eat. I often hid behind the sofa so the bailiffs at the door couldn't see me through the window.

Today, I drive an Aston Martin and live in a beautiful home by the sea, often earning more in one month than I used to in an entire year.

In this book you will discover the steps that enabled me to turn my financial life around. And it isn't just me: my partner, my family and some of my closest friends have also seen their financial lives transformed after following the advice given in this book.

After the success of my first three *Magic* books, *Becoming Magic, Doing Magic* and *Advanced Magic,* I was enthused to write more. The next book was screaming at me to be written: a book about Magical Money. From all the emails I receive, I know that most people are more concerned about manifesting money than anything else. Money has turned out to be the very easiest thing of all to manifest using the law of attraction, cosmic ordering, deliberate manifestation or whatever you choose to call it. I prefer to call it *Magic*. As manifesting money has now become so easy for me, it seemed obvious that I should write a book based on what I knew about the subject.

But I hesitated…

What would people think of me? Would I be classed along with all the 'get-rich-quick' snake oil salesmen? Surely I should be writing about manifesting love or happiness or spiritual connection…

I was also afraid that everything would somehow backfire. Making money from a book about how to make money felt somehow dishonest.

I soon realised that these fears said more about me than they did about those of whose criticism I was so afraid. But I have not yet been able to manifest a different personality – one that is ruthless enough not to care what people think of me. I continued to worry about this. This book began to take shape, but part of me felt I couldn't publish it. Could I really place myself in the same category as all those dodgy moneymaking schemes and hard-sell titles?

I stopped trying to work it out and I *trusted* that the answer would present itself to me. And that's when it came to me:

I would give the profits from this book *back to you*. (Or, at least, to those who matter to you.)

This book is a kind of big thank you to my wonderful, kind, inspiring readers. Of all my various reader groups, you magic bunch are most definitely my favourite! You, who write to me daily with your declarations, your wonderful stories of manifestation and magic, and your well-wishes. You are nothing short of an inspiration to me.

I have decided to give the profits away in the form of a donation to the favourite chosen charity of one of you. You will find full details at the end of this book.

(I had originally planned to give the profits away in the form of a cash prize to one reader, but international red tape made that idea too complicated to be workable.)

As soon as I made the decision to give the profits back to my readers, it was as if a huge weight had been lifted. Suddenly, the worry and tension evaporated. I stopped the mental tussle, and everything freed up, inside me and in the world. The writing became easier, my motivation was high and all was well again in my world. Instinctively, I knew for the first time that I was absolutely doing the right thing in writing this book.

I can't tell you how good it feels to have the money and freedom to be able to give back. Big houses, nice clothes and flashy cars are *nothing* compared to the feeling of being able to help those that matter to you. I have never been so happy in my life, not because I have lots of money and shiny things, but because I make other people happy. So, in buying this book, you are not directly contributing much to my bank balance; but you *are* contributing massively to my happiness…

I hope that's okay with you.

2 Living the Dream

I'm under no illusions here: I know that not every one of you can become rich. If every person in the world became a millionaire, being a millionaire would mean nothing. I'm no economist but I suspect that if everyone did what I am about to show you, the net effect would be nothing at all. It is a fantasy to imagine that The American Dream can come true for every single aspirational person.

But that's fine – because I'm not speaking to every human being on this planet, aspirational or otherwise. Only a tiny percentage of the world's population will ever read this book (or a similar one). An even smaller percentage will act on the instructions that appear in this book, and an infinitesimally tiny number of people will really *live* these instructions, making this plan their own, living it, rather than blindly following. These are the people who *may just make all their financial dreams come true.* So please, make the decision now to be part of that tiny percentage that goes on not just to read, but really to embrace what I am about to teach.

Those who have read my previous books will know that I don't always toe the party line when it comes to manifestation and the law of attraction. Sometimes my advice flies in the face of current New Age dogma. But you should know that I write absolutely truthfully and from the heart; when I give advice in my books, it will never be just to please nor placate my audience, to sell more books or make more money. No, you can trust that my advice always comes from my direct experience and that I take it to be absolutely true.

It is not always possible to give very precise instructions for particular types of manifestation, and I have usually shied away from doing this. For example, I don't feel confident in creating a set of very specific instructions for manifesting a partner, friends or a new job. It's true: I have a manifested a spookily perfect partner and a great set of friends;

but for obvious reasons, I haven't worked *repeatedly* on manifesting these things because my work in these areas is done. On the other hand, I *have* worked over and over on manifesting *money*. I've done it time and time again. In fact, I do it constantly. This means I have a lot of experience of seeing what works and what doesn't. It also helps that money is an almost universal concept, which means we all tend to have very similar thoughts, ideas and problems surrounding it. It is for all these reasons that it is possible for me to give a slightly more specific set of instructions than I usually would.

But please realise that I am simply offering you *one* way to bring money into your life. This is *my* way; it is certainly not the *only* way. I can only write about what I know. My readers have asked what *I* did specifically to completely reverse my fortunes. This book is a faithful account of exactly and only that.

You may also like to consider reading the three books of the *Course in Manifesting* series, *Becoming Magic, Doing Magic* and *Advanced Magic* before we get started. The books are short, and profits from each go to different charitable causes. Reading these titles will give you a good grounding in Magic that may well make your money manifestation attempts more effective; but it isn't absolutely necessary and you should be able to make great progress with this book alone.

Be warned: I don't do 'quick and easy' manifesting books. I don't do tips or tricks. I don't do 'six easy steps'. I give you something else – something that actually *works*. If you are looking for a simple Magic word, a technique, or trick that will allow you to manifest a million dollars by the weekend, you will be disappointed. I don't work like that.

I am *not* saying this will be easy. I'm not saying it will be instant. I *am* saying it works.

This is a *practical* book. It is written not just to give you a self-help 'buzz' and make you feel good for half a day. It was written to bring money into your life. So it's time to move on from reading and motivation to *action*. You have bought this book because you need money, and it's now time to bring *actual* money into your *actual* life.

So let's get straight to the point: In general, when it comes to manifesting money, the initial advice is the same as I have always given.

1. We *prepare* by addressing any negative attitudes (outlined in *Becoming Magic*).
2. We *ask* (not always necessary. Outlined in *Doing Magic*).
3. We *receive*. We let go of wanting and move into the *Magical Receiving State* (outlined in *Doing Magic* and *Advanced Magic*).

From what you have told me, the advice given in those first books is often all that is needed to see a miraculous upturn in fortunes, both financially and otherwise. But when it comes to money, it's not always so straightforward. Money is actually one of the easiest things to create once you know what you are doing, but things can often get 'stuck' early in the process.

It was like this for me. My finances were actually the last thing I mastered 'magically'. Long after every other part of my life had picked up, money remained elusive for some time. I felt cursed, blocked, financially stuck for ages. But here's the amazing thing – having got things right once or twice, I went on to discover that, even after a lifetime of poverty, money turned out to be the very easiest thing of all to manifest using Magic.

And I went on to bring a shocking amount of money into my life.

I sincerely hope I can help you do the same.

As with all my writing, I don't ask you to just accept anything I say without testing it against your own thoughts and experience. There is no benefit in simply sticking religiously to the instructions, as if these words hold some Magical power, like saying 'abracadabra'. It is not performing the steps that work the Magic, not ever. It is the state these instructions get *you* into that makes Magic happen.

So always try to understand the point of each thing I advise. Don't be one of those who just read the words and then declare 'it's not working'. Notice the effect that each step has on *you*, your energy, your situation, and ultimately your finances. As you will hear me say, again and again: rather than attempting to *do* magic *on* the world through waving a wand, carrying out steps or saying a magic word, the way to real success is to *become* Magic yourself and let the world automatically and effortlessly reflect back a life befitting the new you.

So don't just *follow* the instructions – try to *live* the instructions.

Those that understand this point have every chance of *Becoming Rich*.

3 It All Starts With Money

In *Becoming Magic,* I explained that in order to *do* Magic, you must first *become* Magic; that to change your life, you must change *you*. To do this, I advised that you spend some time 'clearing away the dross' – cutting out the negativity, the complaining, the moaning to which so many of us are addicted, and replacing all of this with feelings of gratitude for all the good that is in life. I recommended you keep a gratitude journal to record daily blessings. I know from the letters I receive that these two preparation steps alone (stopping complaining and feeling gratitude) have been life-changing for many people.

When it comes to manifesting generally, erasing negativity is relatively straightforward – we stop idly complaining and gossiping, stop listening to the constant bombardment by negative news reports, do not indulge in bemoaning the state of the world, and we keep a gratitude journal. In doing this, we begin to get into the habit of focussing on only the good in our lives, and begin to filter out the apparently 'bad' stuff.

But erasing negativity isn't always straightforward when it comes to money. After all, so the saying goes, *love of money is the root of all evil.* Complaining and worrying about money, about the economy, about greedy corporations and the effects of capitalism, about the gap between rich and poor – these things are endemic in western society. Many of us even feel we *should* complain about such things, that it is our *duty* to have negative thoughts concerning the desire for money.

And yet we still want it.

In *Doing Magic*, I introduced the *Magical receiving state*. This is the state of non-wanting, of trusting or surrender that allows your desires to flow to you. It is *only* when we move away from asking for what we want, and into receiving, that the Magic really works, and the more time you can spend in this state, the more wondrous your life will be. One big reason that manifesting money can be so difficult is that the negative and/or contradictory thoughts we often have about money can keep us stuck in asking and out of this Magical receiving state. If you are like the majority of people who struggle financially, you will have negative or confused ideas and beliefs surrounding money.

In the pages that follow I will show you how to reverse or eradicate these negative thoughts and behaviours. Rather than flabby advice to 'be more positive', 'be more like this', or 'stop being like that', I am going to show you *practical* ways to make these changes straightforward and automatic.

'But money's not really that important to me.'

And herein lies the first contradiction. Many people I come across tell me 'I don't want to be rich. I just want to be comfortable.' Readers who write to me are often at great pains to point out just how uninterested they are in the pursuit of more money, that they *just* want to clear their debt, or they *only* want to pay off their mortgage, or they *simply* want enough to get a reliable car. One of the main confusions I see in attitudes to money is a conflict between wanting money on the one hand, while on the other hand feeling this desire is somehow beneath them.

Why can we not talk publicly about a desire for more money without adding some sort of justification to prove to everyone how non-shallow we are? Why does it feel so distasteful to act in pursuit of money? Does having money turn you into a bad person? If money isn't a worthwhile pursuit, then why do the poor need more of it? Is money important or not? You can't have it both ways.

So much ambivalence, so much guilt...

No wonder that money can cause such a problem for those starting out with Magic.

In my experience, people who struggle financially rarely have an open, carefree or otherwise neutral attitude to money. Money is the cause of much heated emotion, so many mixed feelings – anger, resentment, bitterness and jealousy. It can destroy friendships and marriages. It can even cause people to kill.

Because of this, manifesting money can have a 'dirty', shallow, unworthy feel about it. Many, *many* people would love more money, but feel they shouldn't… they feel they *ought* to be pursuing less selfish and materialistic goals.

You might not want a Lamborghini, but you would quite like a car that doesn't embarrass you. Perhaps you would just like to buy yourself a few nice things for once. You know that money doesn't make you happy, and that it's not necessary to be rich to have a great life, but still … you would quite like a bit more of it.

Deep down, perhaps this creates a tension in you. After all, you are bigger and better than all this. You aren't one of those shallow people who care for nothing but designer goods and flashy cars. You *want* money but perhaps you feel you *ought* not to. Even I felt this, when writing this very book. I felt writing a book about money was a shabby thing to do, somehow beneath me. The precise way I overcame those feelings will become very important a little later in the book.

So how are we to counter this?

There are many schools of thought and many books that try to teach you that money won't bring you happiness; that rich people often lead shallow and bored lives; that the very happiest people are often the poorest financially. These books advise you to start out by working on manifesting happiness, fulfilment or purpose.

This book is not one of them.

Contrary to some more 'spiritual' books, I recommend that almost *everyone* start out with trying to manifest a monetary goal.

Why?

To explain why, let me tell you a story…

The strangest thing happened to me when I started to become wealthy. Previous to my experience with Magic, I had been struggling financially almost my entire life. I had had difficulties for so long I didn't really know who I was without my money problems. I just didn't remember life without them.

When I turned my attention to money Magic, my financial situation changed rapidly. In the space of about seven months, I doubled my income. 18

months after I had started working with money Magic, it had increased sevenfold.

For the first few months of being wealthy, things were rosy. I began paying off my debts. I bought new clothes, a car and had a lot of fancy meals in nice restaurants. Soon the day came when I realised I was financially independent – I no longer needed to work. I had a passive income of more than enough to pay for my mortgage, my bills and as many nice clothes, cars and meals as I could ever want. So what now?

Seriously…*what now?*

I remember getting up in the morning day after day and not knowing what to *do* with myself. I would answer a few emails, I would surf the Internet in a coffee shop. I would tidy my house and put a load of washing on. I might meet a friend for lunch occasionally. But most of my friends still had to work all day and so weren't often free. At around three p.m. I would end up bored. I actually started playing PlayStation games. After a few weeks I had completed *Bioshock* 1, 2 and 3 and I was ready to go insane.

Sure, I could work more, write some more books, and earn more money so that I could pay someone to tidy my house, do my washing and answer my emails.

But *then* what would I do all day?

For a few months, this caused a bit of a depression in me. I felt conned, betrayed even – all this time I had been led to believe that the pot of gold at the end of the rainbow would be the answer to all my problems. My dreams would all come true as soon as I got my hands on it. But now, I had that pot of gold, and my life hardly felt any different. I no longer had to work in jobs I hated, that much was true. But in its place I had boredom, lack of direction, and some nice things.

It was as if I had lost the driving force in my life. I had lost the *reason* for getting up, working, and going about my life. I realised that money and the lack of it, and the trying to get more of it, had ruled, run, dictated my life for so long that once that had gone, *I had NO purpose in life!* I realised that I had dedicated my life not to doing the things I loved, or finding purpose and meaning, but to the endless, constant pursuit of money. Without that daily pursuit of money, I had no reason to get up in the morning.

Perhaps you have heard about the phenomenon of lottery winners who become really depressed, even kill themselves. I always had considered these simply to be weak, unimaginative people. But now, I completely understood their plight. All my life I had been chasing money, thinking that the only thing missing in my life was enough money not to have to work in jobs I hated. It turned out this wasn't true at all. Chasing money had simply been a distraction – a false purpose, a red herring.

I had heard the old 'money doesn't make you happy' cliché more times than I could remember. But I only realised its truth when I experienced it for myself. I *had* to learn this for myself.

And so do *you*.

Some gurus teach that you should start by working on happiness and fulfilment, bypassing the whole issue of money. They teach that money will show itself to be irrelevant once you have manifested true purpose and are spending your days doing only what you love.

That's probably all true in theory. But in practice, it's just too darned hard to do! How can you begin working on manifesting true happiness, purpose or fulfilment if you are terrified of eviction, repossession or bankruptcy?

How can you find the time and motivation to work on yourself if you are working every hour that God sends in a job you hate for inadequate pay? If you are broke, you probably spend all your time working, you have little time or freedom to do the things you love. You have no time to dedicate to Magic, or to spiritual projects. You try your hardest not to complain, and to stay in a Magical state of trusting, surrender or grace, of not wanting and yearning for money, but it's difficult when the gas bill hasn't been paid and the bailiffs are at the door.

So there is no point in my trying to convince you of just how shallow and pointless a goal chasing more money really is, because you almost certainly won't believe me. You may wish you did. You may have noble aspirations to being one of those who 'doesn't need money to be happy'. But deep down, I still suspect you would like a little more. And here's the kicker - until you actually *have* money, your saying 'money doesn't matter' is mere noise.

Most likely it is something you feel *ought* to be true. No, the only way you can *really* come to see the relevance or irrelevance of money to a really happy life is to become rich and learn it for yourself.

Don't fight the wish for more money in an attempt to find purpose or meaning or spiritual enlightenment. If that desire for money is nagging away at you while you are trying to manifest something nobler, you aren't going to manifest a thing. Don't fight it. Go with it. Manifest the money. Manifest lots of it. Get it out of the way, and then move on to better things.

Of course, these days my life is not boring or directionless at all. I have a wonderful sense of purpose and my life is full of adventure. But I would never have been able to find that purpose and enjoy this adventure until I had freed myself from that constant, nagging worry about money.

This is why I have written a book on making money! It is not until you are free from the shackles of chasing money that you will you be able to decide what it is that truly makes you happy. Make money. *Get rich.* Get that stupid issue of financial worry out of your life, clear the confusion and guilt, and who knows what you will be capable of?

This is why I recommend everyone begin their Magical journey with a monetary goal. Just get that big, fat elephant out of the room and then we can get on to the business of sorting out the rest of your life. Believe me, it is far, *far* easier to sort the rest of your life out when you have the financial freedom to think about something other than survival.

Money itself may not buy you happiness, but it does buy you the freedom to find out what will.

'But rich people are all jerks. I'm worried being rich will make me selfish and arrogant.'

In my experience, the opposite is true. If anything, having more money can make you into a nicer person. When you are no longer obsessed with your own financial problems, you will have the time, freedom and opportunity to turn your attention to helping others.

If you are a caring, unselfish person now, just think how caring you could be with a big wad of cash. When you manifest a lot of money, this doesn't automatically turn you into a mean, arrogant person, concerned only with material wealth. I currently have one car, one home and some of my clothes are ten years old! I have zero interest in designer fashion labels and I would feel utterly ridiculous driving a Ferrari.

Do you want to know the best way of helping those in need? *Get rich.* Get rich and use that new wealth accordingly. When you are rich, you'll see just how much easier it is to help others. Before becoming wealthy, my charity donations consisted of £20 once or twice a year to a TV campaign, and buying a Big Issue magazine at Christmas. These days, I'm in a position to be able to give around 50% of my income away. That's not something I could have even considered doing while I was still struggling.

Let's flush out and try and lose all those negative connotations that money often has, and instead focus on all the good that can come from becoming rich. If you are currently a kind and helpful person, you will be able to show your kindness and helpfulness to a much greater extent when you have money, freedom and time to do all the wonderfully good deeds that are currently locked inside your head.

PART ONE

Learn How You Get it Wrong
So That You Can Get it Right

4 Lottery Wins, Surprise Inheritances & Chests of Treasure

I discovered New Thought and the 'law of attraction' decades ago. For over ten years I attempted to bring money into my life using affirmations, vision boards, visualisation and other 'new age' manifesting techniques. And for over ten years I got things horribly, disastrously wrong. Like many people who struggle financially, I was convinced that the journey from poverty to wealth would go like this.

Step 1. Poverty

Step 2. Win lottery, inherit a fortune, or invent Google/Facebook

Step 3. Wealth

So I hung pendulums over lottery numbers. I bought copies of *Country Life* and drooled over the photos of million-pound homes. I covered vision boards with photos of supercars. I had big, big ambitions and as I saw it, there was only one way for someone like me to get one of those homes and one of those cars. I was convinced that winning the huge Euro lottery jackpot was the only way out of poverty for me.

I know from the letters I receive, and from people I speak to, that many other poor people think this way too.

Let's look at what *doesn't* work, so we can figure out why, *and fix it.*

I'll now describe the way that many people (including me for many years) attempt to manifest money.

Think of a truly enormous sum of money, probably this will be millions or billions but certainly it is enough to solve all your problems, allow you to follow your dreams and never to have to work again. Next, flood your mind with thoughts of your goal, do affirmations and visualisations of your new life. Imagine yourself walking around your huge luxurious multimillionaire's house, visualise taking your new Maserati for a drive, imagine the feel of the leather steering wheel, fantasise in the greatest detail. Sit and wait and wait for the money to appear. Alternate your focus between thinking of your huge goal, and all your current money worries. Think about money, or the lack of it, constantly.

If a bit of unexpected money does appear, go out and spend it all immediately to treat yourself (after all, that's what rich people do). If a piece of bad financial luck appears a few days later become immediately despondent and hopeless. Pick up another book and revisit manifesting again, focussing this time on this weekend's lottery draw. When you don't win, resent and feel bitter toward the person that does. Become despairing, perhaps wondering why you never get the breaks when all those rich people seem to have it so easy.

Repeat the process.

When the millions still don't appear blame the writer or creator of the plan you have been following or dismiss the whole idea of Magic and the 'law of attraction' as a scam.

Give up and declare it doesn't work.

Be honest, is there *any* of this that resonates with your experience? Are any parts of this story similar in any way to your own manifestation attempts? Because I can promise you, something very like this story was my experience for many years.

So what's wrong with this, specifically?

Although there will be subtle variations and exceptions, there are several common reasons that people find money so difficult to manifest using Magic or the law of attraction. And if you have been unsuccessful so far, I suspect that one or more of the following has been true for you:

Problem 1. You have gone in too high, putting random huge demands to the universe for millions or billions. *You have gone for your biggest desire too soon.* You have set out, without *any* prior experience with Magic, and tried to manifest a million right off the bat.

Seriously, if it really *were* as easy as that, *we would all be rich already!*

42

Problem 2. You have never truly let go of the grasping wanting, not for one second. *So never entering the Magical receiving state.* People who want to manifest money usually want it like nothing else in their life. They yearn and dream about having money. Money may seem like the answer to all their problems, the only thing standing between them and an exceptional life. As I will explain later, this desperate want, this constant asking and associated focus on *lack* is a big part of why they never manifest it.

Problem 3. You have put out your demands for more cash, but haven't put out a changed, 'rich' persona into the world. You haven't taken any steps towards being the person you want to be. You continue to think, feel and act just like before, waiting for the money miraculously to appear. *So not becoming a person befitting your chosen manifestation.* In other words, you have been *attempting to DO Magic on the world, rather than BECOMING Magic.*

Problem 4. You feel bitter, jealous, angry or resentful toward rich people. You may be concerned about social issues, poverty, the gap between rich and poor and feel these are to blame for your own financial situation. *So not taking complete responsibility for your life and/or situation.*

In the remainder of this part of the book I will explore these 'problems' in more detail. This will allow you to watch out for them as you progress. But don't worry if you suspect these troublesome issues are present in your life, because in part two I will give you a practical way of dealing with all of them.

5 The Magic of Thinking Small

Some of the very poorest people in society spend large proportions of their salary or welfare benefits on lottery tickets and scratch cards, thinking this is the only hope for them to escape their predicament.

It is so very sad that those in greatest need cannot see another way out of their predicament. Because I truly believe there is almost no chance of people like this winning the lottery jackpot. Sudden, enormous windfalls for the very poor are infinitesimally rare. This is not just because the statistical chances are so low. It is because the universe doesn't allocate anything according to need, but to your entire being, to the person you *are*. And I believe encouraging people to go for the big desire, the million dollar manifestation, no matter what your current financial state, just adds to the problem.

In *Becoming Magic*, I encourage you to see Magic less as something you do, and more as something you *are*. We set out on the Magical journey, not by trying to 'make things happen', but by working on ourselves, by *becoming Magic*. We work to become more like the kind of person who already has our desires in life. I am fond of advising you to stop attempting to do Magic *on* the world, as if it were something you could pick up and put down. Instead, I advise you to take steps toward becoming the person you want to be, and then watch in wonder as the world magically changes in step.

In the past, I tried many approaches that on the face of it, seemed to suggest something similar. I tried to follow advice such as this:

'Act like a millionaire and you will become one.'

'Fake it 'til you make it.'

You know the type of thing I'm talking about. For example, I read that a great idea is to make an appointment to look around a sumptuous mansion that is for sale and imagine yourself living there, or to take your dream car out for a test drive, just to get used to the feeling of driving a millionaire's car.

I was *entranced* by this idea. I decided I would put on my best posh accent, bite the bullet, and book a test drive in an Aston Martin. The universe was *bound* to notice that! All I needed to do was take that dream car out for a drive and the lottery win would be mine.

Unsurprisingly, it didn't really turn out like that; so, at least for now, please don't book a test drive in a supercar.

Why?

If you're the type of person who is used to driving nice cars, used to taking hugely expensive cars for test drives, and feels completely comfortable and confident in that situation, fine – you will probably thoroughly enjoy the experience. If you can bluff your way into convincing the garage you are a serious buyer, fine – you may feel genuinely motivated by taking a £100,000 car out for a drive. But if you don't feel *completely* comfortable all this will do is draw sharply into contrast just how far you are from truly owning that car. If you are lacking in confidence and feel in any way intimidated by the idea of taking a Ferrari for a test drive, *don't do it.*

Because here's what really happens when an insecure person follows that standard New Age dogma and books a test drive in a car that is way out of their reach.

You turn up at the garage on foot, having parked your old car around the corner so the salesmen can't see it, and walk nervously into the showroom. A salesman comes smiling towards you to shake your hand, takes one look at your cheap shoes and your slightly battered, five-year-old handbag and his demeanour changes. He can tell in an instant that you aren't a genuine buyer *because you don't feel like a genuine buyer*. His smile drops and his expression turns to one of faint contempt. *You shouldn't be here.* The salesman takes you on as short a drive as courtesy will allow during which you drive slowly and nervously, feeling insecure and inadequate. *You don't belong here.* On returning to the garage, the salesman takes the keys, locks the car, and immediately walks away from you back to his desk. *He isn't taking you seriously.* And you walk, shamefaced, back to your fifteen-year-old heap of junk, dejected and angry. As you may have guessed, this is exactly what happened to me when I first test-drove an Aston Martin.

How was I supposed to manifest anything in this state?

This experience set me back for the longest time. I felt I simply wasn't the right kind of person to drive that sort of car, or to be rich and successful. All this experience did was draw sharply into focus just how gaping was the chasm between my goal and my current state of lack. I actually had that horrible feeling of *I'm not good enough.* It was a real low point in my life.

This is why I'm advising you *not to go for your biggest, shiniest goal up front.*

I *know* some other writers tell you to think big, to go for the big desire, to work on manifesting a million up front. After all, the universe doesn't care whether you ask for $5 or $5 million; it's all the same.

It's just as easy to manifest a million, as it is to manifest a penny.

I totally disagree.

Manifesting a million or a penny may be all the same to the universe, *but it's not all the same to you!* If manifesting a million seems like an impossible dream, then right now it *is* an impossible dream. The chances of your being able to manifest a million from a place and mind-set of poverty and desperation are just tiny.

I don't care how many times you have been told to imagine your dream home, your dream car or your castle in the sky. Looking at the dream just draws sharply into contrast how far you are from that life. It shows up acutely just how much your current life is lacking.

In *Becoming Magic,* I demonstrate that the world reflects the person you are, not the things you ask for. If at the moment you are not a millionaire-kind-of-person then you don't have a snowball in hell's chance of manifesting a million.

And if you *have* experienced the manifestation of a large windfall from a place of desperate poverty, the chances are it left you again rapidly and dramatically. Am I right?

So what is the answer?

When it comes to Magic, and *particularly* money Magic, I am a big fan of starting small; slowly, gradually but *solidly* and *reliably* increasing your trust in your own power and your ability to bring wonderful things into your life.

So first of all: stop looking forward to a hypothetical, mythical time when you are a multi-billionaire, walking around your mansion looking at the rich furnishings. Forget the fantasy in the clouds for a bit; I want you to think closer to home. Let's deal with the here and now.

Before mastering Magic, I was living a hand-to-mouth existence. I was bringing in around £1300 (around $2000) per month. But I had £30k worth of credit card debt and a huge overdraft. My outgoings were crippling. I worked all the hours I could packing products in a local factory for minimum wage just to be able to pay the bills. Most of the workers at the factory were economic migrants from Eastern Europe. Some of these people had lived in true poverty and had hungry families back at home they were sending money to support every week. Women workers would often burst into tears because they were missing their children so much. These workers were used to working much longer hours, in poorer conditions and for far less money. Because the migrant workers were so glad of the work, I think the management of this factory used this as an excuse to treat us badly – almost like animals.

In a twelve-hour shift, we were allowed only half an hour for lunch and two ten-minute tea breaks. These short breaks were the only time we were allowed to sit down. This meant we were standing for over eleven hours out of twelve. We were not allowed to speak, take extra toilet breaks, or to slow down production for any reason. (I eventually walked out after an incident where I was reprimanded – for *laughing!*) I often thought the company would have used slaves, if only it were legal.

As you can imagine, I wasn't exactly a millionaire-kind of person at this point.

I had already had some success with Magic but not with money; for some reason, that still eluded me. Writing was the only thing I had any talent for. I had a couple of books out already but the sales were dismal so far. I knew I was never going to win any prizes for my books, but if I really put some time into writing, I might be able to eke out a living as an author. But I had no time for more writing because I had to work such long hours in the factory. I felt completely trapped. Strangled by debt, I scraped by like this for years.

But it was during the long, boring hours at the factory that I began to really study Magic. With nothing to do with my mind all day, I had all the time in the world to think, plan, listen to the odd audiobook, watch people, react to people, try things, and record everything that happened at the end of the day in my journal.

As I reflected, not on *what I had read*, but *on my own experience*, I began to discover things, insights, truths.

I, like so many others, had been lured in by the Magic of thinking big. I had tried to manifest a million pounds so many times, and failed.

When I really began to understand how Magic actually worked, it became obvious why I hadn't been successful.

I had set my sights too high from a place that was too low.

I had already seen the evidence of the way Magic works in other areas of life: Magic is something you *are* not something you *do*. You attract a life that reflects the person you are; not the wants you have nor the things you deserve.

Well, I may have *wanted* a million and I may have felt I *deserved* a million; but the universe wouldn't care about that – it would just see the person I was: *me* – poor, unorganised, worried about money, obsessed with my financial woes, working in a factory for minimum wage, not a millionaire kind of person at all.

So what possible reason would the universe have for bestowing riches on *me* out of all the other billions of voices asking for a lottery win?

I had had enough of all the pie in the sky promises of The Law of Attraction. So, I gave up all notion of the lottery win and the Magic of thinking big. I forgot about trying to become a millionaire.

Instead, I devised a plan, a path, a way of bringing all I knew about Magic to the specific area of money. I was going to get it *right* this time – not looking to the clouds, but to *me* and where I was at that moment. This meant starting small, *with what I had.*

I remember having the idea that if only I could sell ten books a day, I could earn another £1000 a month. How *amazing* would that be? I could then pay most of my bills with the royalties from my books. *That* wasn't too far away from my current state. It was entirely believable and so achievable.

I put my Magical plan into action. The book sales picked up and I achieved this first goal very easily indeed.

The logical next step was thinking that if I could just sell 30 books a day I would earn £36,000 a year. I remember thinking that this would be completely life-changing; it would be more money than I had ever earned in my life, all from book royalties. I could give up working in the factory and focus full-time on writing.

This too, didn't take long to achieve.

From that significantly wealthier place, my next dream was to earn £100,000 ($150,000) a year. The funny thing was, the idea of earning 36k, which once seemed like a wonderful fantasy, seemed like *nothing* once I had 100k in my sights.

When I hit 100k, it just felt 'normal', 'right', 'obvious'. £100,000 didn't even seem like an enormous sum of money anymore. Because I had become a £100,000 a year-kind-of-person.

So how did I do it?

Well, I didn't jump from rags to riches overnight by focussing on a mythical lottery win. No, instead I just *gradually* became the person who fitted the life I wanted.

In order to do this, I focussed on, respected, was grateful for, and dealt appropriately with *what I had* not *what I wanted.* In doing so, I was able to feel, think and act ever so slightly richer *right now.*

And noticing that I was behaving in a more sensible, non-needy and organised way around money (just like a rich person), the universe gave me a little bit more.

And I began to live from that new, slightly wealthier place. I respected, was grateful for and dealt appropriately with the money I was given (just like a rich person). I ate in slightly nicer restaurants and drove a slightly newer car. I began to feel, think and act like a slightly richer person.

And so the universe gave more again, and so it went on, getting easier every time. As it became easier, the momentum gathered and money started to flow easily to me. Within around seven months of starting this Magical money plan, the factory was a distant memory, the snap-backs had ceased and my income had doubled. *Doubled!* Around one year after beginning, it had increased sevenfold. I had gone from earning minimum wage to being one of the richest people I knew.

But I couldn't have got here without taking the intermediate steps.

I am sure that if I had set my sights on £100k a year when I was packing boxes in a factory, ripping my fingernails and straining my back, being treated like a packhorse just to pay the electric bill, *nothing would have happened!* After all, at that point I just wasn't a £100k a year kind of person. I had to get used to having 20, 30, 40k and dealing appropriately with that amount of money before the universe would let me have more.

And here's the delicious and slightly unfair thing: when you become a rich sort of person, creating more money becomes *effortless.* It flows to you, you become lucky, you get all the breaks, you bounce back from any adversity. You just become a rich person all round.

You'll become the person who walks into that Aston Martin garage (as you may have guessed, I do love Astons) and just stands there and waits as the salesmen rush over in their fight to serve you. They will ingratiate themselves to you, not disrespect you. You will have *genuine* confidence – not that kind of 'fake it 'til you make it' contrived confidence. And when you do, you will not let anyone intimidate you ever again because of a perceived lack of money.

And *genuine* confidence with money doesn't come from fantasising, or from visualising, or even from suddenly becoming rich. It comes from gradually, solidly, genuinely *feeling* richer.

So stop dreaming of the lottery win. Stop yearning after the castle and the Maserati. Let's stop focussing on what you *want* from a place of lack.

Instead, let's get *you* right. Let's change *you* and watch the money flood in all on its own. Remember, life doesn't reflect what you *want*. Life reflects the *person you are*. If we change *you*, the world will begin to change automatically to fit your new persona. We have to shift your focus away from what you *want* (and therefore lack) and instead focus on what you *have*. The richer you can feel *now, with what you have,* the more the universe will reflect riches back at you.

Get that right, and watch in wonder as everything else begins to fall into place.

So forget the Magic of thinking big. I'm far more interested in the Magic of thinking *small!* By thinking small, I may never have won the lottery....

But I *did* manifest a million pounds.

6 Asking for What You Want

So where does asking fit? When do we get to ask for all the lovely things we really want?

In my other books, I have included specific techniques for the purposes of asking the universe. However, asking is not only usually unnecessary; it can often cause more trouble than it's worth. And believe me, if you have had a lifetime of lack, *the universe already knows what you want!*

So this time, I'm going to do something a little different. I have decided not to include a section on asking techniques at all. In fact, when it comes to money, I suggest you miss out the *asking* part altogether.

One of the most important ideas I teach in all my books is that *want* is equivalent to *lack*, and that our desperate grasping, our constant *wanting* and *asking* keeps our desires from ever manifesting. By continually focussing on your wants, you inadvertently end up focussed on everything you lack, on everything you *do not want*. It is our constant asking for things, or for things to be different, that keeps us stuck and prevents our desires from ever coming to us.

Most people remain stuck in the *asking* state their entire lives.

The fact is, asking is probably the least important part of the whole process. It is only when you move away from *asking* and into *receiving* that you get what you want. You will know this to be true already if you have ever had that infuriating experience of a goal coming to you once you stopped wanting it.

The way to manifest easily is to bask for long periods in what I call *the receiving state*. This is a state of trust or surrender where we are *not focussed on our wants at all*. The receiving state is as close to a situation of *non-wanting* as is possible for us.

In *Advanced Magic,* I take this notion of non-wanting one step further, in suggesting that to make your Magic more efficient and powerful, you must find a way of being okay, truly okay, with every little thing that occurs, *even with the non-manifestation of your desire.* Paradoxically, your desire is then all the more likely to come to you.

Hence I am certainly *not* an advocate of those approaches that suggest you write your goal on a piece of paper, read it 100 times a day, create affirmations around it, flooding your mind with thoughts of your goal, *asking* constantly, perhaps hundreds of times a day. This constant asking will only work to keep that goal from you.

I am also bemused by advice that says that to manifest successfully, you must get really, really clear about a goal you want, and then ask that it appear *by a definite time,* advising you to focus on some very specific particular thing occurring, by some very specific particular date.

I just don't understand how this can work. It seems to go against everything I know about Magic.

The way to successful manifestation is to let go of wanting to the extent that you almost don't mind whether or not this particular goal even happens. Making such precise, specific and repeated demands cannot possibly help.

You may have noticed that no matter how many times you have asked for a desire, no matter how much you have visualised it, or created affirmations around it, it hasn't come to you. This is because by asking, you are still wanting. And by wanting, you are generally focussed on all that you lack.

Nowhere are you more likely to end up focussed on lack than when you work on money goals. The more desperate you are for money, the greater the gap between your current financial state and where you want to be. The greater this gap, the more likely it is that you will end up focussed on and fretting about your desperate state, rather than where you want to go.

Before discovering Magic, I spent most of my life planning the day when I would win the lottery. Before we had a national lottery in the UK, I used to imagine winning the football pools, or the premium bond jackpot. I imagined this 'winning' day in vivid detail hundreds of times. Probably for over thirty years I visualised this day.

Someone would turn up at my house to deliver the news. I would invite them in to my house so that the neighbours would not overhear. I would go into town and buy a new outfit, get a taxi to a nice restaurant, order Champagne and then just sit and think about what to do next, letting the news sink in. Then I would gather my family and tell them that I had just signed a big business deal and that all our lives were going to change. I wouldn't tell anyone about the lottery win.

That dream was so clear to me; I ran through it so often in perfect, vivid, intricate detail. I could almost taste it.

But it never materialised.

No matter how often and how clearly I visualised it. No matter how much I thought about it. No matter how much I asked for it. I never won the lottery.

Of course, not *all* goal-setting is a bad idea. If you have a goal to sell 1000 products in a month, I can see that precise goal-setting and an exact, clear vision could be very important. But any attempt to *force* something to happen by a particular date and time will, by its nature, destroy any Magical element.

So how do you balance the idea of working towards an actual, physical goal – such as a big work target, and yet employing Magic at the same time? It sounds like the different methods interfere with each other. Can we only use one or the other?

The truth is, I set actual, physical, tangible goals all the time...sort of. It might be to sell a certain number of copies of a particular book, or to write a certain number of books in a year. I do this constantly.

I am just really playful with it.

For example, I don't do this sort of goal:

"I WILL DO ANYTHING AND EVERYTHING IN MY POWER TO ACHIEVE 1000 BOOK SALES PER DAY BY THE END OF THIS YEAR OR DIE TRYING. THIS IS MY SOLEMN VOW, SET IN STONE FOR ALL ETERNITY AND MAY GOD STRIKE ME DEAD IF I FAIL."

Talk about making things hard for yourself!

No, my goals are a bit more like this:

"I'm (caps lock off, this time*) planning to get to the point of selling 1000 books a day and have fun doing it. I trust fully that whatever happens along the way will be success, or will be a stepping-stone to something greater. As long as I'm enjoying the process I don't much mind what does happen."*

The first sort of goal, though very precise, would achieve *nothing.*

The second goal, though rather vague and woolly, would be almost certain to come to fruition.

While writing the book you are reading at this moment, I decided to set an absolute deadline (very unusual for me). I decided that for the sake of portent, cosmic significance and general spookiness, I would release this book on 21st June, the Summer Solstice – an important date in some people's Magical calendar. But it turned out that trying to force the Magic to a deadline only acted to ruin things. The writing became slow and torturous, my mind became fuzzy, and everything stopped feeling like fun. As the deadline approached, I pushed even harder, deciding to dedicate every day between then and the deadline to writing. I would do everything in my power to publish on that date. But things just got worse and I began to feel really bad about the book. I couldn't publish. I didn't know why, but something wasn't right.

So I stopped trying to force things. I let go of the supposed importance of that silly date and decided to let the book take just as long as it needed to. In fact, I stopped writing altogether and went away for a weekend to the wild Suffolk coast, one of my favourite places on earth, to clear my head. And it was in Suffolk that I came up with that idea to give the profits back to the readers.

So *that's* what the delay was about! Now I knew why that arbitrary deadline had been wrong for me. If I had forced this book to be published on 21st June, I would never have come up with that idea, and this book would have just looked like yet another of those 'I'm making tons of money pretending to teach you how to make money' books. So instead of having a book I would have been faintly ashamed by, I have a book I am genuinely proud of, all because I let go of a deadline and let things take their own sweet time.

According to one opinion, I had missed a deadline, I had not achieved my goal. I had *failed*. But I take a different view. By letting go of the deadline, I simply moved onto the correct path. These days, I never fail to achieve goals. Because missed goals are not failures. They are just pointers to something better.

So please try to let go of the idea that money must come in particular amounts, in a particular way by a particular time. Let go of the idea of precise asking, of exact and clear demands. The more precise your demands, the more likely you will be to see *any* apparent diversion from your idea as a disaster.

But what about those times when you need money, really quickly, by a certain deadline? Sometimes people write to me to ask what to do about an imminent financial disaster. For example, they want to know how to manifest $10,000 before a certain date to avoid going bankrupt or being repossessed. They might be about to be evicted from their house unless they can raise the outstanding rent in a few days.

I'm really sorry, but I don't know how to do this. I have a recipe for riches, but not for *instant* riches. There is good reason for this. The way to *all* successful manifestation is to let go of the grasping wanting, to drop the asking. For a person desperate to raise 10k by Friday, that state of non-wanting is nearly impossible to achieve.

If apparent financial misfortune comes along, *refuse* to view it as bad or as evidence of things going wrong. Look for the silver lining, *always* – remember, this is just a stepping-stone to something greater. Look to the positive and try to see an opportunity for growth or learning or movement in a new positive direction. Sometimes the positive direction will be obvious, sometimes the stepping-stone will be clear; but at other times you may never find out *why* some apparent mishap came along. If you can't see the silver lining, just trust that it is there. Finding out the whys isn't the important thing here. The important thing is to move your attention to the positive, even when financial 'misfortune' comes along. Because in doing this, you stop wanting things to be different, you stop asking for things to be different, you trust and *believe* that everything is turning out just right *and this is the perfect state for manifestations.*

Let it all be. It's all good. Don't make demands of life. *Dance with life* and it will lead you on a wonderful adventure.

Let's sum up my advice on asking for what you want. Those of you who are familiar with my other books, or otherwise have some successful experience with Magic, can go ahead and use asking techniques if you really want. You *can* ask in quite specific terms and still be very successful, *as long as you let go of asking rapidly.*

But if you haven't read my other books, don't worry, because you'll probably do better without using an asking technique. Moving out of asking and into receiving is hard enough at the best of times. For any of you who are completely new to Magic, it's going to be near-impossible when dealing with the very thorny subject of money. Money is the graspiest, neediest, wantiest, askiest desire of all! And until you can be a little more proficient with Magic, I say *to heck with asking.*

So, for this book, we don't ask at all.

7 What is this 'Receiving State' You Keep Mentioning?

In my *Course in Manifesting* books, I teach that *receiving* is far more important than *asking*. I introduce you to the concept of the Magical *receiving* state – a state of trust, love or surrender, a state of non-wanting that allows Magic to flow into your life.

This Magical receiving state is variously described as one of 'letting go', of 'surrender', of 'getting out of the way of manifestation'.

I personally like to access the receiving state by using the notion of *trust*.

When I make the decision to *trust*, absolutely and completely, I accept that everything, *everything* is working out just right. I let go and stop trying to make things happen, safe in the knowledge that everything is being taken care of for me. In this state it actually doesn't matter whether or not I achieve my goal because I trust that no matter what does unfold, it is exactly the right thing for me. When I *trust*, I stop trying to make things happen; I stop wanting things to be different. I stop trying to *change things*. I *have* no attachment to any outcome, not even to the thing I am attempting to create.

As I often say: *wanting* could almost be viewed as the opposite of *having*. If you would like to change something about the present moment, e.g., desiring more money, it means you are *wanting things to be different*. And if you continually want things to be different, this will effectively block all your manifestations.

In *Becoming Magic*, I encourage you to take steps towards kicking the complaining habit – something that is very strong in most of us. Let me be clear: complaining about a cold meal, unsafe working conditions, or an inaccurate bill are obviously valid forms of complaint. What I urge you to eliminate is the complaining that is done continually, for fun or to pass the time of day. Often this is done quite unconsciously and you may be astonished at how often you find yourself complaining once you start paying conscious attention to it.

Every time you complain, you are publicly declaring your dissatisfaction with some part of your life. To enter the receiving state, you need to feel as happy, satisfied and grateful for your life as possible. This is why I recommend everyone take steps to reduce or eliminate complaining. Another great idea is to keep a gratitude journal in which you record moments of happiness, contentedness or gratitude at the beginning and end of the day.

The less you are judging the current moment as unwanted, or feeling a desire to change things, the more content, accepting, and grateful you feel. Thus the world reflects more things back that make you feel content, accepting, and grateful. The more you can feel accepting of the present moment, *the faster your desires will come to you.* If you want to read further I suggest you try *The Power of Now* or *A New Earth* by Eckhart Tolle, or my own *Advanced Magic.*

But here's the kicker...

GENEVIEVE DAVIS

It can be *extremely* difficult to stay in this state of profound non-wanting when dealing with money. If you have severe money worries, it can be *so* difficult to stay in the correct state of *trust* day to day. No matter how positive a person you are, your money troubles may be clouding your every thought; your life circumstances may keep nagging constantly at you, reminding you of just how far you really are from your goal. When you have strong money worries, letting go of wanting more money, just *trusting* that every little thing is working out just fine can feel like an impossibility, even for a second. You want money fast, and you feel that want every moment of the day. And this constant need and desperate grasping want only acts as an effective 'block' on our manifestations and keeps money from ever coming to us.

When it comes to money, an ideal way to achieve this state of non-wanting which I've already touched on is to begin thinking, acting and speaking like a rich person – *as if* you were someone who knew that money would come to you easily, *trusting fully* that everything was working out just perfectly, as if you were someone who didn't need money, as if it really didn't matter

76

one way of the other, as if you already *had* plenty of money, as if *you didn't even really want it.*

I know what you're thinking: how on earth are you supposed to achieve this? Many of us don't have the first clue about how to act like a rich person. How can you act rich when you have old clothes and not a spare penny to spend? How can you manifest a million when you have no idea how a millionaire acts, thinks or feels? How can you 'be okay' with the possibility of the non-manifestation of money when your current financial situation is very much *not* okay? How can you let go of *wanting* money when the lack of it is interfering with everything in your life and colouring every thought?

The good news is, I'm going to show you an easy and fantastically effective way of doing exactly this.

8 Taking Ultimate Financial Responsibility

Nowhere is taking responsibility more important than when dealing with money.

However, this is where I start to tiptoe. It is this very subject that has led to yet another delay in my publishing this book, even when it was all finished and ready to go. I know this section is necessary, but I also know that some will not take well to what I am about to say.

It is almost a taboo subject, particularly here in the UK, to suggest that those in poverty should have any part at all to play in escaping their own misfortune. This is what makes it so hard for me to write the following:

I believe that each and every one of us is ultimately the only one who can sort his or her own life. I believe the *only* way out of poverty involves taking absolute, complete and utter responsibility for improving your own financial state. There, I said it.

Now, this issue of taking responsibility is the bit that usually gets people fired up. This is where some like to leap into action, indignantly shouting 'but that means you're blaming starving children for their own poverty!'

This is a complete misrepresentation of what it means to be responsible. I want you to see that there's a massive difference between *blame* and *responsibility*.

The existence of starving children is not an argument against *your* taking control of *your* own life. It's not as if becoming empowered somehow means you are a bad person. It's not as if by taking responsibility for *your* life, you somehow force children to starve!

I completely agree that wealth certainly is *not* dealt evenly and things are not 'fair'. Some of us are born into enormous privilege, some into terrible poverty. But some are also born healthy, some ill or disabled. Some are born beautiful and strong, some plain and weak. Some are born into abuse, others into loving families. We don't all start at the same place. Some have it incredibly easy, others have it really hard. Things happen. Life isn't fair. Footballers and bankers earn too much, nurses and teachers don't earn enough. More should be done for the very poor.

This is all true.

But one fact remains over all this.

There is only one person who really has the power to change *your* financial misfortune – and that person is *you!*

Taking responsibility is absolutely and utterly vital to doing Magic for this simple reason: every time you blame *someone,* or *something* for your bad luck *or* your misfortune, *you give your power away.* In order to do Magic, you must become Magic. And you will never become Magic if you are focussed on changing the wrong thing.

Blame the world for your misfortunes and you will never change them.

Credit the world for your good fortunes and you will simply continue to dismiss them as luck.

Society may owe you something, your boss may owe you, your government may owe you, I don't argue with any of that; but sitting around doing nothing, waiting for richer people to share their money with you, or waiting for the government to sort out your life is like starving to death because it's someone else's turn to cook. We can chat about injustice until the cows come home, but it's not going to change your money woes.

Idly complaining may even make your situation worse.

The world you experience is just a reflection of the person you are. We do not do Magic 'on' the world, but we must *become* the person we want to be and watch the world shift in step. This is why we must *become* Magic before attempting to *do* Magic.

Now, think about the kind of person you become when you feel you are *owed* something, when you are a perceived victim of injustice. Think about the persona you put out into the world. Feel the emotion that comes up. It is *horrible*. It feels like burning resentment, bursting anger, desperate longing, with possibly even a touch of fear.

What do you think you might manifest while in this state? Do you think the world is going to send you money while you are feeling constant injustice? Is it going to reflect back a new life of riches and luxury? Highly unlikely.

Crudely put, every time you criticise the rich for being rich, feel jealous of those with more than you, or blame the government or your boss for your money problems, you don't *change* your financial situation, *you perpetuate it!*

If the very rich really *did* want a secret way of keeping money from you, the best way would be to reinforce the prominence of this notion of the 'haves' and 'have nots'; to keep up the focus on the growing gap between rich and poor; to keep you in a state of victimhood with a feeling of burning injustice, because *that* would be the surest way of keeping you from ever being financially comfortable.

Casting people as victims works very effectively to keep them powerless. By keeping them focussed on all the bad in their lives, it leaves them eaten up with resentment for an entire lifetime and prevents them from taking those first steps toward an exceptional life.

Can you now see that taking complete responsibility is the most empowering step you can take, catapulting you out of victimhood and allowing you to begin creating and controlling your life in positive and exciting ways? When you take responsibility you take *control!* You take power. You take your life off its present mediocre, negative course and turn in the direction of success, happiness and wealth. You are no longer in a battle between 'them' and 'us', between 'rich' and 'poor'. In fact, you are not even part of that dynamic any more. You are on your own path now, you are telling a new story – *your own* story.

Change the world, by all means. Help people in any way you can. Try every day to make the world a better place. But don't imagine for one minute that you can change the world (or your own finances) from a place of resentment, jealousy or from a sense of injustice or entitlement.

Victimhood is helplessness. Responsibility is power.

Responsibility can be a scary thing. Some of you have even told me you are *afraid* of being rich. Others feel that to be rich would somehow change them, that they would 'lose touch' with their roots, that their friends would come to resent them. Some don't feel *worthy* of being rich. Some have even told me they feel they don't *deserve* money.

(If you are one of those who feel unworthy of financial success, I recommend you read *Becoming Magic*. It might just reignite your natural, inherent magnificence and give you a sense of your own Magic. Once upon a time, perhaps in childhood, you may have felt invincible, immortal, and capable of anything. In *Becoming Magic* I try to reignite that Magical spark – doing my best to show that everyone and anyone can be powerful, inspiring, and exceptional.)

We need to find a way to take the confused emotion out of money. I want you to begin to see that money has no inherent ethical dimension whatsoever. It has no necessary emotion or mood attached to it. Money is a big nothing with no meaning beyond a simple means of exchange, one thing for another. Money is an abstraction. It is neutral.

Yes, people do fight and kill and behave badly in the name of money. But people also fight and kill and behave badly in the name of love, in protection of their families, their friends, and *certainly* people act badly in the name of their religion or their god. But this does not mean there is inherently anything bad about love, family or God.

From being someone who thought about money every second of the day, I have slowly developed what I describe as a 'respectful neutrality' to money. I don't see myself as part of that rich/poor them/us dynamic any more. Money is something I use, when I need it.

My car won't run without petrol. When it is out of petrol, I go and buy some.

I can't stand coffee without milk. When I'm out of milk, I go and buy some.

My life runs more easily with money. When I need more, I go and make some.

Money is not the be-all-and-end-all, it just makes some things run better, and getting more of it has no more emotional baggage than getting another pint of milk.

It is this neutrality that I believe is a large part of my financial success. Because this neutrality means I no longer really mind how things turn out. And not minding how things turn out is the absolute key when trying to do Magic. Being okay with every little thing that happens is the key to an exceptional life.

'But earlier you questioned those who claim money isn't important. Aren't those people just naturally neutral when it comes to money?'

The fact is, if someone really *were* neutral about money, they probably wouldn't be reading this book. They would never have picked it up in the first place. What I see in the people that write to me is a *claim* that money isn't important, coupled with a desperate desire for more. As I've said earlier, the only way to find out how important money really is to you, as well as the only way to truly feel neutral about money, is to get lots of it.

It's very easy for me to tell you just to drop any neediness, guilt, resentment or confusion around manifesting money. It's all very well telling you to stop resenting the rich, or to let go of your desire for money; but in practice, all these things are easier said than done, especially if you have had a lifetime of lack and of thinking a certain way. My just telling you to stop *being like that*, stop *thinking like that*, well, that isn't going to help you one bit. The question is, *how* are you supposed to change your thinking?

In the pages that follow, I'm going to show you a simple way of doing exactly this.

9 A Little Preparation

Before we get started, I'm going to ask you to commit to making a few preparations. My first book, *Becoming Magic,* is dedicated to the single purpose of preparation – getting *you* into the right state for beginning Magic. From all we have discussed so far, it should be obvious why these steps are important. If you like, you can read *Becoming Magic* before you start, but it's not strictly necessary as long as you commit to the following steps:

1. Make the decision to take complete responsibility for improving your own financial state.

2. Make a commitment to not complaining about money or your finances, not *ever*. If you find this very difficult, you might like to read

A Complaint Free World by Will Bowen. It will change your life.

3. Keep a gratitude journal. Have a small notebook in your pocket, briefcase or purse and write down three things, morning and evening, for which you are grateful. Try to feel the emotion of gratitude as you do so. If 'gratitude' does not mean much to you, try having a 'Why I'm so happy' or a 'Good things that happened today' journal.

Even if you follow just these three steps, you will change your life in incredible ways.

And having made these preparations, and having seen how things can go *wrong,* let's now turn to getting things *right.*

PART TWO

Getting it Right

The Two Steps to Becoming Rich

10 Step One:
Do it for Them

My first recommendation is that you start out on your money Magic journey by manifesting *for others*.

This is not so that I can stroke my own ego, assert my moral superiority, and boast about all the charities I support. And it is not because it's the 'right' thing to do, according to some arbitrary moral compass. No, it's because manifesting money *for others* could make your first attempts at money Magic more successful than they might otherwise be.

It may well be that you find great happiness in buying bigger and better cars, fancier clothes and sparkly diamonds; but even those who love the specifically material trappings of wealth are likely to find greater success when they incorporate *giving* into their manifestation attempts.

I promise you: by making your actions and your projects at least partly charitable in nature you will open the floodgate to riches.

How?

Previously, I introduced you to the idea that constant *wanting* and the associated focus on *lack* stops us from *having*. Remember, the universe does not allocate riches according to who wants or deserves it the most. It is the grasping, desperate yearning for money that ensures it stays beyond our reach.

Giving is about as far away as it is possible to be from grasping, desperate, yearning *want*. The emotion in freely giving is on the opposite pole, being closer to love and gratitude than to anything else.

Giving completely reverses any resentment you may also be feeling. By tuning your focus from your own sense of lack, toward those who lack *more* than you do, you instantly remove any sense of 'entitlement' or bitterness towards those who *have* more than you.

Giving is in some sense 'spiritual'. By making your manifestations charitable, you no longer need be held hostage by feelings of 'money isn't a worthy goal' or 'money isn't really important' or 'I should be trying to manifest something more than mere money'.

Giving is also massively *empowering*. Just think about that quantum leap from being the one asking or begging to being the one who is *giving*. You are not a beggar or a needy victim – you are a bestower of riches, a philanthropist, a creator, a *white knight of justice*. Believe me, this is about as far away from victimhood as it is possible to be!

No matter how poor you are there will always be someone that pulls at your heartstrings. It may be a particular organised charity, or it could be a family member. It may be the homeless man who always says hello on your way to work, or the street children of Rio. It could be your own granny who needs a hip replacement operation, or your mum who has always wanted to go to Paris but has never had the money. You might consider sponsoring a child in a poor country so that you have some personal connection with the recipient of your charity. Find someone, or some group of people or even animals that 'get to you'.

Now imagine being able to hand over a life-changing amount of money to them. Imagine how good it would feel. For most of us, this is far more motivating even than sorting out our own financial situation. Think about the energy of the emotion of *giving*. Think about how good it would feel to help someone about whom you care deeply.

Instead of all those negative money thoughts, you are filled with feelings of love and a light-hearted, excited, motivated desire to help. You have a direction, *a purpose*.

Sometimes, people write to ask me whether their choice of charity is a good one, whether it's okay for them to give money to their best friend, or to an animal charity or even a political party. They write, it seems, asking for my approval. Should they instead be giving to *Save the Children*, *The Red Cross* or *Oxfam*?

In my experience, your charity donations must be to a cause that *matters,* to *you personally*. So don't just plump for a random faceless charity that means little to you. Don't forsake the cat's home you love because *Save the Children* seems more worthy.

Give to your church *only if it feels really good to you.* No one has the right or authority to tell you your cause is not worthy, or that theirs is more deserving. If you give blindly to charity, no matter what it might be, your giving isn't going to have the desired effect. In doing this, you will effectively be 'giving only in order to receive'. If you give under duress or a feeling of obligation, you also aren't going to achieve the desired state. Rather than basking in the receiving state, you may well end up feeling resentment and ambivalence to the whole process of giving, and the Magical aspect of giving will be wiped out.

I never feel pressured or guilt-tripped into giving for charity. If anyone demands a charity donation, I won't give it unless I am moved to do so personally. Some will disagree with me but I feel that charity must be freely given and with love and compassion. No matter how worthy the cause, if it is bullied, persuaded or guilt-tripped out of someone, it is no longer charity but extortion. The collectors in the street who use clever sales tactics to garner donations (much of which goes to paying their own commissions) will never get so much as a penny out of me.

'I would love to be able to help others eventually, but I am in such dire straits that I really need to sort out my own problems first. It makes me feel bad that I need to put myself first.'

Look, there is nothing wrong with working on your own financial state first. You may well be able to be successful by manifesting for yourself before you turn to helping others. And don't ever feel bad or guilty for doing so. Feeling guilty will only serve to pollute your own Magic.

I am most emphatically *not* on a moral crusade.

All I am saying is that for most people, manifesting money seems to work better and is easier when done for someone else. I'm not saying you should send all your money to the third world when you have holes in your shoes. I'm just saying that that by incorporating *giving* into your manifestations you may get your new shoes all the faster.

'But not everyone has become rich by helping others. Don't you agree that there are rich, ruthless businesspeople who exploit the poor?'

Of course I agree. Some of us don't need to give in order to receive. Some very successful people are truly ruthless and uncaring. Some are cruel and despotic; some are arrogant megalomaniacs. Some are happy to let the poor starve while they become richer. It is not just the good and kind who become rich.

But this is not who you are, is it? If you admire rich, despotic leaders and ruthless, exploitative businesspeople, then it's possible that you too can create huge sums of money by acting in a similarly selfish way.

But if you feel any sense of discomfort in being ruthless, selfish or exploitative then it's going to be impossible for you to create money by acting like this. Your own conscience will only get in the way, *every time*.

Personally, I don't think this has anything to do with some sense of universal 'balance' or karma. My own hunch is that the answer lies much closer to home, deep within us. I believe in karma, but not as an external power, energy or yardstick. I believe karmic justice comes from within.

Besides bypassing any negative emotional baggage you may have, I think helping others brings good into our own lives because deep down, we *believe* this is right. Deep down, we don't feel good about having something for nothing, or for taking without giving or for having lots when others have nothing. Deep down, I believe *most* of us have this moral sense of the need for balance in the world.

Indiscriminate *taking* without giving back creates a sense of unrest, of discomfort, of things not being 'right', of being 'unbalanced'. This is a killer for manifestation. By *giving*, we redress any imbalance that might have scuppered our manifestation attempts.

In short, manifesting money for others works so well because it bypasses a lot of the negative beliefs and attitudes we consciously and subconsciously hold about money. Manifesting for others completely reverses the focus and breaks the logjam that you have built up over the years. All those feelings of poverty, loss, inadequacy, resentment, fear, worry, longing, injustice, jealousy, yearning… all these are bypassed.

Instead we access feelings of compassion, warmth and true self worth. Giving thus automatically takes us closer to that Magical receiving state I'm always going on about – the state of *love, trust* or *surrender* that allows your desires to enter your life. This is why I believe giving results in more getting. *Giving* freely and with feeling and love (*not* resentfully and simply in order to receive something back) gets you into the perfect state for receiving money.

This is Magic.

11 When Money Controls You:
The Horror of The Financial Snap-Back

In my case, I never really had any great feelings of resentment towards the rich. I envied them and thought they were somehow 'different' to people like me, but I didn't hate them for their money. I never thought that manifesting money was shallow, selfish or materialistic.

No, my biggest problem with money was quite different.

While I was growing up, my own mother would use the phrase 'we can't afford' it several times every single day and she frequently spoke of 'living on the poverty line'. Looking back, her story wasn't really true. Money was very tight for us and we never had new cars or holidays, and sometimes the phone would be cut off when my mother couldn't pay the bill. But we never went hungry. 'Living on the poverty line' was just an exaggerated description of a fairly average upbringing. But the effect of this story was not good. I grew up imagining I was one of the very poor ones, belonging to that most unfortunate of social classes – the 'have nots'.

I think part of me felt that I simply wasn't one of those who ever *could* have money. I don't think I really *understood* money. It was like politics, or particle physics – very important perhaps, but it was the preserve of *other* people, different people, *rich* people.

Money was just not something I was able to have, understand or cope with.

I am a terribly disorganised person by nature, and nowhere was this more apparent than in my financial life. For the first forty years of my life, I had no control over my spending, no system, no planning. Most of the time I didn't even know how much I earned, let alone how much I spent. Saving money didn't even come into the picture.

Somehow, each month the bills got paid and I got by. Some months, chaos ensued and I would get completely lost and out of control. Most of the time, I simply ignored my piles of unopened bills and avoided sight of my bank balance. As if by not acknowledging the disaster that was my finances, it didn't exist.

Yet I thought and worried about money about 90% of the time. Part of me thought that by hiding from money, I would be safe. But my life proved another story. In my refusal to take control of money, I had allowed money to control me, completely and in almost every moment. I was obsessed with money and was desperate for more of it, yet at the same time I was terrified of it. I was terrified of having it, of not having it, of receiving it and of losing it.

No wonder I found manifesting more money so difficult in those early days of using Magic. My finances and my attitude to money were pure chaos.

In *Becoming Magic* I wrote about the snap-back. This is the sudden loss or turning sour of a large and fantastic manifestation. Sometimes, when we have seemingly performed the perfect

105

manifestation, some other thing appears in our lives to negate it.

It seems to be the case that snap-backs happen particularly with financial matters. When people manifest a big sum of money, they very often lose it by way of a huge unexpected bill, or similar sudden expense. I hear this again and again when people write to me. Addressing this problem was one of the main motivations for writing this book.

You may find it reassuring to know that I had a long history of terrifying snap-backs. Whenever I did manage to manifest money it would leave me, spectacularly. I would manifest a wonderful sum of money, and a huge unexpected bill would come along – a car repair bill, a vet bill, a tax bill – and wipe out that money. Or I would decide to pay off my debts, a big chunk of them. Three months later, the debts would be back where they started and more.

Whenever money came, it left. And I never, ever felt I had any control over it whatsoever. This left me frightened to work on manifesting money at all, and I came to see Magic, and particularly money

Magic, as just too powerful and unwieldy, too unpredictable and chaotic for me to deal with.

The worst of these snap-backs happened after I divorced. When my ex-husband and I sold our house, we received far more money than we ever expected for it. My half was more money than I had ever had in my life. I received £110,000. I was a relative newcomer to the law of attraction and New Thought at this point and didn't really know what I was doing. Like many complete beginners, my first manifestation attempt was successful and I was completely elated at how easy it had been. I remember the day I paid the cheque into the bank, feeling like my life had truly begun.

I don't really understand what happened next. I did buy a small car, and went on a nice holiday. But other than that I don't really remember what I spent. What I do know is that within months, all the money was gone.

A few months more and I found myself with £30,000 of credit card debt with almost nothing to show for it. How on *earth* had I spent £140,000 (around $210,000) in less than a year?

I'll tell you how.

Several huge and unexpected bills came along to wipe out large portions of it. But there was more than that at play.

I treated this money with no respect. I blew it here, there and everywhere. I spent some, I lent some and I lost some. I made random financial decisions and bad spending choices. I had absolutely no plan and no idea how to go about using it, spending it, saving it, or making it work for me. I was simply not used to handling that much money. I didn't really know where to start. I was all over the place. I didn't act like a rich person at all. I acted like someone who isn't used to having money in her life.

I wasn't a rich person.

I was just a poor person with money.

And so, the money left me...

I want to make sure there is no chance of this ever happening to you. I want to not only enable you to manifest money – that bit is easy – I want to also enable you to *keep it*.

Ironically enough, this awful snap-back turned out to be the greatest stepping-stone ever. Because now

I *knew* Magic was real. This sort of thing had happened to me far too many times to be explained away any more as mere coincidence. Something was going on. *Magic* was going on, and this time, I was going to master it.

I am going to show you a way of controlling money, and never ever letting it control you again. It will be at your behest, under your direction, your power. You will have the power to wield, use, control, receive, spend money. You will never be scared around money again.

To master money Magic, you need to show the universe that you are someone who is capable of looking after money and spending it sensibly. You need to cultivate a healthy, professional, non-needy, non-resentful, non-fearful attitude to money. You need to 'become rich' *first* and let the world reflect back a life befitting the new you. If you can do this effectively, money will come to you *and it will not leave*.

And how do you do this?

Slowly!

12 Step Two: Becoming a Rich Person Before You Are Rich

If you don't become the person befitting your manifestation, it will almost always leave you.

Remember, a mirror won't smile before you do; but when you *do* smile, a mirror will faithfully and accurately reflect that smile back. Become the person you want to be and the universe will reflect a reality back at you that is consistent with that person. When you can become the kind of person that has your desire, your desires will just gravitate to you.

You need to become a rich person… who just happens to have no money. To do this, you need to learn to *feel, act and think rich.*

There are two sides to being rich. One is the physical aspect of actually having the cash. The other, more important aspect is those thoughts, feelings and behaviours that accompany being rich. These are more important because they are what attract the money to you in the first place; theses are what keep it from leaving you; these are what keep it flowing to you. Without them, you really are stuck waiting for a lottery win. The good news is that we can work on these other aspects long before the money actually starts to arrive.

Acting as if you are rich works because it enables you to let go of your wanting, just a little. You don't feel the lack as keenly. You don't spend every waking moment thinking about and yearning for money.

Now, you may have heard this sort of 'fake-it-'til-you-make-it' advice before in other books. While the advice to 'act rich' is sound, in some sense, it's not always that helpful in itself.

You see, for many people trying to manifest money, their present state of being is so far removed from that of a rich person that they don't have the *first clue* about how to shift from this place and begin acting like one.

After all, how on earth can you think and feel rich when you don't have two pennies to rub together?

You'd love to act rich, but you don't have a spare penny to spend on rich purchases. You try to think rich but all around you is evidence to contradict those thoughts – the unpaid bills, the old clothes, the hole in your car exhaust that you can't afford to have repaired. You take a dream car for a test drive and end up humiliated (as I so painfully did). You can say 'I'm a millionaire' as many times as you like, but somewhere deep down there's always a little voice saying 'No, you're not. You're absolutely flat broke!'

Many years ago I worked for a *very* short and *very* unsuccessful term in a life insurance office. My boss was very into sales psychology and was always going about spouting *'think like a millionaire, talk like a millionaire, act like a millionaire and you'll become a millionaire'*.

My boss's millionaire advice never worked for any of us in the office. But that is not to say there isn't truth in his little saying. It's just that we had no idea of how to act, think or talk like millionaires. The problem was, we assumed that acting rich meant one thing: *spending*. After all, rich people spend all their time buying expensive things, not worrying about the cost or the consequences, so we thought. So, to act like a rich person, the answer is to buy lots of big expensive things, yes? Use credit cards, if you like; after all, the money will come soon.

Big, big, *big* mistake.

For us (and perhaps currently for you) acting like a millionaire just meant spending all our money haphazardly without any worry about the future repercussions. After all, this is what millionaires do, isn't it?

No, it's not. The opposite of poverty, or of 'I can't afford it' is not indiscriminate spending. Indiscriminate spending is a killer for financial success. Spending haphazardly is what sudden lottery winners do – those who go on to lose their entire fortunes. It's what some celebrities do – those who go on to become bankrupted by their tax bill. Genuinely rich and successful people are organised and sensible with their money. They spend, and they spend big. But they do so within limits, even when those limits are very high. Above all, rich people treat money sensibly, calmly, and *with respect.*

But if the key is to start acting and thinking differently around money, how on earth is this going to happen until you get some of it?

You can't think rich thoughts until you have money... ...and you won't have money until you think rich thoughts.

You can't act like a rich person until you have money... ... and you won't have any money until you act like a rich person.

Someone once said *the secret to making money is having some.* This is absolutely true. But it's not just because money can be used to invest and so make more. It is because having money makes you feel and act richer, and when you feel richer more money comes to you. It is because, (like every other thing you try to manifest) the more desperate you are for money, the further it stays from you. Once you have money and no longer need to manifest more, it will come to you by the bucketload.

Horribly ironic, unfair even, I know. Forget what you read in the papers: this is the true poverty trap!

I'm going to show you a way out of this Catch-22 and gently break you out of that vicious circle of poverty thinking – a way of easily feeling, thinking and acting a little richer *before* you have a lot of money. In this way, you will let go of some of your frantic wanting for money and in doing so you will more easily access and *stay* in the Magical receiving state for money.

No lottery wins here, no instant millions. But little by little, bit-by-bit, inch-by-inch, we are going to make you rich.

13 Let's Make you Feel Richer

What exactly is a 'rich thought'? What do rich people think about? Many of us have never had a rich thought in our lives and wouldn't even know where to start.

So in order to get the ball rolling, rather than trying to think rich thoughts out of nothing, I'm going to give you things to *do*, things which will make the rich thoughts happen spontaneously and decrease the poverty thoughts. You could say it's a practical and non-Magical way to make *Magic* happen.

I am going to show you a simple way of feeling less anxious, less needy about money. I am going to show you a practical way of *acting* richer, *feeling* richer and so automatically *thinking* richer, with no more than the money you have now.

Get it right *with what you have* and the universe will *notice*.

So, let's begin making you feel rich. What in your life makes you feel rich? For most people, it is spending. Most people think the only time they can feel rich is when they are buying things. But here is ironic lesson number one – to feel rich, you need to place just as much emphasis on *saving* as you do on *spending*.

Now, I *know* that you probably don't feel you have a single penny to save, that you spend every penny you earn on food and living; you may even spend *more* than you earn each month.

I know all this; I was there once. But keep reading.

What is your greatest problem with money? Are you constantly wrong-footed by sudden expenses? Do bills come along and wipe everything out, just when you thought you had got in control of your finances?

Or do you never have any money for big things like holidays, or new cars or TVs? Do you use credit for these things and then regretfully spend months or years paying them off?

Or do you never have any spare cash for life's little luxuries? Do you let your hair grow long and unkempt because you can't afford a good haircut, or buy poor quality clothes and cosmetics? Can you not remember the last time you spent any money just on yourself?

Or do you feel completely out of control with your finances. Do you feel overwhelmed, panicky, even frightened around money?

Or do you feel all of these?

We are going to change all of this.

I am going to introduce you to a very simple money-management plan, the value of which goes far beyond mere practicalities or organisational benefits. Even if you are very familiar with money managing I think you will still find my take on it extremely interesting.

I first came across simple money managing from reading other books such as *Secrets of the Millionaire Mind* and *The Richest Man in Babylon*. There are dozens more books written on the subject. I fully admit that the nuts and bolts of this particular idea are not remotely original to me. Wherever you

119

look, someone seems to be talking about money managing.

However, I find it bewildering that for more than 2000 years financial experts have been writing about the benefits of managing your money, but almost all seem to be skirting around the issue regarding why this really works.

Money management simply means separating out portions of your current income and allocating each share for different purposes and expenses. And for some proponents of money management, that's as far as it goes; this is just a savings plan – saving in one area just frees up money in another.

But in concentrating only on this very practical aspect of the plan, these other writers have left out the best bit!

They have left out the *Magic!*

Without being told about this Magical dimension, you may well have rejected the idea of money management as too austere, as only for rich people, or as otherwise irrelevant to you.

As I always say, it is not the Magic wand, nor the technique, not the affirmations nor the vision board that works the Magic. These things are inherently powerless. It is the state these things get *you* into that works the Magic. It is their effect on *you*, it is their ability to get you into a particular Magical state; it is because they allow *you* to become Magic.

As far as I can see, money management is just another of these devices, like saying affirmations or doing a visualisation. But this particular device works on one sort of manifestation *only*. It works on money. And perhaps *because* it is so specific, it is one of the most awesomely powerful Magical devices there is.

In itself, money-management doesn't work Magic. But the effect it has on *you* can bring miracles into your life.

When I first decided to pick myself up from the packing factory, and to change my life once and for all, I looked at my life and what I had managed to manifest so far. I had manifested a perfect boyfriend and a wonderful social life plus thousands of other smaller things. But I had never managed to achieve that same success with money. Manifesting other things was relatively easy now, but money was still elusive. And when I did manage to get my hands on a big sum, it generally left me quite rapidly.

So I looked at the successes I had already had. What had worked so well with the other manifestations? What had I done differently when it came to money? And then I realised – in all cases, things generally came to me once I had stopped yearning and asking for them. But I hadn't even *begun* to stop asking for and wanting money. In fact, it's fair to say that I was I was silently asking for money about 90% of my waking life.

When I had first heard about money-management many years previously, I completely dismissed it. I thought it sounded complicated and boring. I also thought it was out of the question for someone like me. How could I possibly save money when I had so little? Really! These people couldn't possibly understand how difficult things were for someone as poor as I was.

But this idea kept on showing itself to me. Every book and website I read seemed to mention managing, separating, and allocating money for different purposes.

So I read a little more, and gave it a little more thought. And that's when I saw the truth – that money management was the gateway to this 'receiving state' that I was now beginning to understand, to losing my fear and obsession with losing money, to achieving a sort of 'respectful neutrality' toward money rather than my current grasping and confused feelings of lack.

I came up with a plan, distilled from what I had read and from what I already knew to work from my own experience. My partner and I both started on the plan immediately. After a few tweaks and changes I came up with the recipe I present to you now – the recipe I still use to this day. I still follow every step of this even though I now have more money than I could ever need. After all, if I stopped all this now just because I am rich, that could 'break the Magic'.

14 The Mechanics of the Plan

First, you need to set up four separate bank accounts in addition to your normal checking or current account. If you use online banking, this is usually as easy as pressing a few buttons without even needing to go into a branch. If you get paid in cash, or it is difficult for you to set up online accounts, you can use four labelled moneyboxes or piggy banks.

When you get paid, whether weekly, monthly or randomly, you will separate your money into these accounts or these moneyboxes. How much you put into each depends upon your present financial circumstances.

FOR THOSE WHO ARE VERY SHORT OF MONEY:

If you are living absolutely hand-to-mouth, or have almost no disposable income at all, you should do the following:

Take 1% of your take-home salary, wage or benefit payment and put it into account 1.

Take another 1% and put it into account 2

Take another 1% and put it into account 3

Take another 1% and put it into account 4

Leave the remaining 96% in your current or checking account or in your wallet. This is the money you will live on during the month.

FOR THOSE WHO ARE STRUGGLING BUT COPING:

If you are getting by, but rarely have any spare cash at all, if you stay in control of you bills, but have little extra for saving or luxuries, you should do the following:

Take 5% of your take-home salary, wage or benefit payment and put it into account 1.

Take another 5% and put it into account 2

Take another 5% and put it into account 3

Take another 5% and put it into account 4

Leave the remaining 80% in your current or checking account, or your wallet. This is the money you will live on during the month.

FOR THOSE WHO ARE COMFORTABLE BUT NOT AS WEALTHY AS THEY WOULD LIKE:

If you have a reasonable income and some disposable cash each month, you should do the following:

Take 10% of your take-home salary or wage (or dividends that you take from your business) and put it into account 1.

Take another 10% and put it into account 2

Take another 10% and put it into account 3

Take another 10% and put it into account 4

Leave the remaining 60% in your current or checking account or your wallet. This is the money you will live on during the month.

In each case, the remainder of your money goes into your normal bank account or into your purse or wallet and is used for everyday living and bills. If you plump for the third option and decide to put 10% into each account, you will now be living day to day on 60% of your current income. Even if you have a decent income, you may well need to economise quite a bit to manage to live on this reduced amount.

Don't panic! This is going to sound like nothing more than a particularly strict and unpleasant austerity measure, but it's really *so* much more than that. So if this all seems to be taking a rather non-Magical turn, don't be put off. Keep reading. It gets so much better…

It is absolutely fine to start with a lower percentage and build up. But don't automatically assume that 10% is impossible for you right now. Don't plump for the easiest option unless you feel it would be literally impossible to save more. You may be surprised at how achievable 10% is for you.

Ideally, you want to get to the stage where you are putting the full 10% into each account.

From now on, the money in each of these accounts is only to be spent on specific purposes. Some will be saved, some will be spent, some will be given away.

Account 1 is for **BIG PURCHASES**

This is a savings account designated only for large purchases: cars, holidays, new computers or big expensive things that would take you several months at least to save for. You do not spend this money on anything other than large purchases. It is not for everyday expenses, buying normal work clothes, nights out, or impulse purchases. But other than that, you are free to spend this on anything or anyone you want. You can save up for specific things and buy them when the account reaches the required amount; or you can save it up in readiness for a large purchase that you may desire in future. This account is designed to give you experience of the feeling of saving in a disciplined way for long-term large purchases. *Never again will you put such purchases on credit.* You will soon experience how wonderful it feels to purchase such things outright, using your own hard-earned and carefully-saved money, rather than using someone else's money and then spending months or years regretfully paying it off.

Account 2 is for the **FUN PURCHASES**

This account is set aside for frivolous purchases just for yourself, to be spent only on things for *you*, things that make you feel rich, pampered and spoiled. It must never be used for bills or everyday expenses.

Account 3 is a **FOR OTHERS** account

This is where to save for the charity, cause or person you have decided to support. It's usually a good idea to allow this account to build to a certain level, perhaps $100, $200 or $1000 before you give the money away to your chosen charity or cause. You can call this your 'Granny's operation account' or your 'starving orphan account' or your 'hungry kitty cats account'. By referring to it in this way, you will be reminded of how much you are helping your chosen charity every time you deposit money. This will help you to make you feel loving and grateful, gladly and willingly helping others that are less fortunate, rather than resentful at being forced to give your money away.

Account 4 is for **YOUR OWN CHOICE**

You are free to choose what that fourth account might be used for and it will differ according to your particular circumstances.

To help you choose, you need to think about what else might be important to you, financially speaking. What is your greatest financial concern? Is it securing your future? Is it being wrong-footed by sudden expenses? Is it saving for your child's school fees? Is it paying off debt?

Here are some examples of different purposes to which you may put your fourth account:

An Emergency Bills account

A Debt account (to pay off your credit cards or mortgage)

A second charity account

A University or college fund for your children

A home deposit account

A Long term 'Golden Goose' investment account, designated for investments that will grow and bring in an income or make you richer.

Initially, my own fourth account was an 'Emergency Bills' account. This was essential for me because I am so disorganised with my finances and almost every month I would be caught out by unanticipated expenses. If you are more organised an Emergency Bills account may not be important to you at all.

If you have made the decision to raise a very large amount of money as quickly as possible for your charity, you could also use the fourth account to save for this purpose in addition to your 'official' charity account. This might be important if you are trying to help an elderly or sick relative, or to pay for something that has a deadline.

The 'Golden Goose' account is money specifically designated for saving for creating a financially secure future, or to allow you to retire early. Some other writers consider this account to be the most important of all. It is only to be spent on investments; things that will increase in value or that will bring in an additional income. The Golden

Goose account has only one purpose: making you richer. You don't touch a penny of this money unless you are paying for something that is very likely to increase your wealth. In short, this money is *only* to be spent on making *more* money.

You could invest in premium bonds, savings accounts, Forex, stocks and shares or build a fund to buy property. I am not an investment expert – so get advice if you feel you need it.

I never had a Golden Goose investment account until relatively recently because for a long time my priorities were to pay off debt, and to ward off sudden big unexpected bills. I couldn't even think about the long-term future because my main money troubles were more immediate than that. I have now set one up because my immediate financial problems have been solved. I can now look much further ahead. If you are less concerned with immediate issues and more with securing your future, or your retirement, the Golden Goose account may be very important to you.

In all cases, the purpose of the fourth account must be your choice. It must relate to your own life and your own financial issues. It doesn't matter much what that purpose is, as long as it makes you feel richer, more in control and that it helps to solve a current financial concern of yours.

But at the end of the day, it really doesn't matter whether or not you have this, that or the other fourth account. Don't lose sight of what we are doing here in an attempt to get these accounts 'right'. Don't get into a mental tussle about this. As long as you are spending, saving and giving in controlled and measured amounts, it doesn't much matter what any particular account is designated for.

15 How Does it Work?

'But this isn't Magic, it's just economising!'

At first, perhaps like you, I couldn't quite see how separating money into different accounts would do anything other than force me into saving. And how could I save when I couldn't even pay the bills I currently had? I was barely coping with my current outgoings. What sort of life would I have if I had to economise further just to squirrel away a few pounds? Things were tough enough already without further cutbacks.

But I soon came to realise that even if the practical side of money management wasn't particularly Magical, the consequences of it certainly were.

Money management works on two levels. First, and most obviously, the physical separation and allocation of your actual cash into separate portions for different purposes helps you to avoid overspending in certain areas – and so helps to keep you from losing control of the money you *do* have. Like any austerity measure, it frees up money in certain areas by economising in others.

But this is only the rather unremarkable beginning…

Let's be clear here: there's nothing Magic about saving money and putting it into bank accounts. If you currently earn UK minimum wage, and if you didn't spend your Big Purchase savings for a whole year, you would still only have *at most* around £1000 to show for all this economising. That's not going to make you rich! If this book were just a way to get you to save £1000, it wouldn't be worth the paper it was printed on.

So don't view this as a savings plan. Try to look beyond the mere mechanics of organising money. In my experience, those who embrace only the practical aspects of the plan are those who tend not to stick with it, to cheat with the accounts, become unmotivated and give up. Those who embrace the Magical aspects tend to *keep at it*, all the way to riches.

So, I want you to see the practicality of organising your money in this specific way as a tool, as a *device, as a Magical ritual*. Look for the effect of money managing on *you*, for the state it gets *you* into. *This* is where the Magic comes in.

At first, you may well not be able to cope with saving the full 10% into each account and may have to start with the minimum of 1%. Because if you *could* put away 40% of your current income, *just for one month*, something amazing would happen.

For argument's sake, let's say your take-home pay is £1000. You put £100 into each of your four accounts. You economise as best you can, having a really lean month. It's a struggle, but you manage to get by on the remaining 60%.

After one month, you will log on to your Internet banking, or check your balances at the bank or count your piggy banks and find you have £400 in savings! You will have £100 set aside for emergencies or you might have paid £100 off your debts. You will have £100 Big Purchase Money to go towards a future dream. You will have £100 to give away to your loved ones or a charity dear to your heart. And best of all, you will have £100 Fun Money to spend on *you*.

And the universe *will notice!*

Next month, you separate your money once again. You pay off a bit more debt, you buy yourself something nice; you put money toward a future big purchase. You give some money away.

And the universe *will notice!*

Then, after just a few months of careful money management, your whole financial situation will have changed. Every time you look at your bank balances you no longer see empty accounts. Your tummy does not sink at the sight of all those zeroes and negative balances. Instead you see four accounts *all with money in them.*

You will have had a *very* tough few months but the change in you will be amazing. You will now feel sorted, organised, freer. Your money worries will be slightly lessened. You will not feel quite so poor. You will feel slightly more in control of your finances. Your thoughts will not be quite so full of worry and lack.

And the universe *will notice!*

Next time you fancy a manicure, a gorgeous handbag, a bottle of Champagne with dinner, or a shiny new electrical gadget, if there is money in your Fun account *you can have it* without any pangs of guilt or having to justify your purchase, *and so you will feel richer*.

Rather than putting big purchases on credit and then feeling guilt and regret, you will save for these things in advance in your Big Purchase account. Those purchases will be all the sweeter, knowing you actually have the money set aside for them. Your debts will reduce and no new ones will be created, *and so you will feel richer*.

You may already have started giving to your charity, or you may be letting the money build up to a delicious amount, to be handed over when it reaches your desired sum. *Giving* diverts the focus from your own money worries, *and so you will feel richer*

If you have a Golden Goose account, you will place yourself in the small minority of people who actually have invested in securing their future, *and so you will feel richer*.

If you, like me, choose to have an emergency bill account, you will know that next time you have an unexpected expense, there is at least a buffer of cash to cover some of it, *and so you will feel richer*.

Look what we have done. With just the same amount of money coming in each month, we have made you feel richer.

And the universe *has noticed!*

Because money management helps you to avoid panicky situations where you have no money for a certain purpose, you naturally stop thinking about your money woes and so stop inviting more of them into your life. It allows you to do all the essential things to keep money moving and flowing – saving, spending and giving in an organised and sensible manner. It gives you permission to spend money on yourself on frivolous and extravagant purchases. Not in an uncontrolled and irresponsible way, but like a rich person would – sensibly and within limits.

·

Money management forces you to act, think and feel like a rich person.

Instead of pie-in the-sky thoughts of lottery wins coupled with desperation and resentment, the universe sees a new you – a 'you' that is relaxed about, and in control of your money. A 'you' that is acting and thinking more like a genuine rich person. And it will begin to reflect a life back at you that is more fitting to this more organised and financially adept you.

In short, it will send you money.

It's true that you could probably have a lot of success with simply managing your money with *no* mention or attention to the notion of *Magic*.

But you may feel very differently when you have your first experience of 'Magical money' coming to you. When a sum of money comes out of the blue, from an unexpected source, from a place over which you appear to have no control, you may not be so keen to dismiss the notion of Magic.

To be honest, it doesn't much matter whether you believe this works by Magic or by some other means. I like to describe this with Magic, you may prefer some more conventional explanation and that's fine. But don't let the fact that I am calling this particular technique 'Magic' stop you from using it in the first place.

Because *it works*, no matter what you want to call it.

For me, the addition of the notion of Magic to this essentially practical plan powers things up. Magic makes *you* feel special, rich, enchanted, powerful. And perhaps most importantly, it makes you feel less needy, *less wanting*. This state is *perfect* for manifestations. Without the addition of Magic, the whole thing can feel like a chore. 'Magic' takes money managing from being rather austere budgeting to an enchanted ritual.

This is not just a way to help you control whatever amount of money you currently have coming in. It isn't just that by squirreling away little bits each month you will have a slightly easier retirement (we all know people who have done just this and not become remotely wealthy). It goes way beyond that.

At first, it may only feel like a trickle and be almost imperceptible. But keep up the money management until it becomes a fun habit. Commit to 3-6 months of strict money management, follow the rest of the advice in this book, and I can guarantee you will see *more money begin coming to you*.

It will soon become difficult to explain your new-found wealth *without* some mention of Magic, Cosmic Ordering, or Law of Attraction. No matter how sceptical you are now, when everything starts to work, you will start to genuinely to believe that something else *must* be going on.

Then the day will come when you receive your first unmistakeably Magical money – an unexpected sum will come to you – something which once would never have happened to 'someone like you'.

So when some unexpected money comes your way (and it will), don't dismiss it as luck or remark at how unusual this is for you, or how it will 'probably be gone in no time' or that 'it will only just cover the outstanding electricity bill'. Instead, make a conscious decision to see it as evidence that everything has changed for you and that this is just the beginning of a huge upturn in your fortunes. Be surprised, but not *too* surprised! After all, these are the sorts of things that happen regularly to rich people.

Smile when you find a note hidden in your purse or wallet, or a pound in the pocket of an old jacket or on the pavement. Don't ever, *ever* explain these things away as coincidence or luck. Always, always explain these things as evidence of your new money-attracting ability, your new rich status.

So *when* money comes to you, *don't, whatever you do, explain it away.* Whether it is finding a penny on the road or a £50 lottery win, choose to see it as evidence that Magic is working for you. The more faith you have in the system, the more rich and in control you will feel and so it will work better. Do this consistently and I promise you, these little financial miracles will increase in frequency and in amount.

And from now on, *manage every penny that comes to you.*

For some, the effect of money management is almost instantaneous, and they see an immediate improvement in their finances. It was like this for my partner, Robert. It was almost as if the decision to start managing alone changed his financial world. I had also convinced him to change his thinking from constant lack and longing, to thoughts of affluence. I had already shown him that his lifetime of resentment towards rich people wasn't helping him. But it was the money management and the action of giving a percentage to charity that changed things so quickly for him. Just saying 'change your negative attitude' isn't much help to anyone. But giving someone a practical way to make this happen automatically is massively powerful, as it was with Robert.

Before starting this system Robert was claiming housing benefit because he had become unable to pay his rent in a tatty shared house. As a photographer, he had spent 20 years eking out a living selling photographs in online stock libraries, often for pennies each. As he changed his attitudes and the money management started, so did the offers of paid work. Fast forward two years and his income had increased tenfold and he is driving a new BMW. The work offers went from doing badly paid favours for friends to huge contracts from big international companies. He now picks and chooses his clients, working *when* and *if* he likes.

The change in my partner's financial situation was so dramatic, it makes more sense to describe it as involving Magic than anything else.

In my case, things changed a little more slowly. Three months after starting managing money, it felt like nothing much was happening. I felt more in control of my money, safer and so a little richer. But materially speaking, other than the little bit of money in my various accounts, not much had changed.

And then, one day I received an email from a Russian publishing house asking for the translation rights to my first two books. They offered an advance of $4000. All I had to do was say yes; I had to sign my name on a piece of paper and $4000 would be mine. It was not a life-changing amount but this was my first money 'miracle' and it knocked me sideways. It felt as if money had literally fallen out of the sky.

Of course, I could have just put this down to coincidence – my books were good, and this sort of thing happens regularly to good writers. I could have chosen to believe this had nothing whatsoever to do with separating my money or with 'Magic'.

But that's not what I did at all. I chose to see this as absolute proof that the Magic was working.

I didn't blow the $4000 on a fun purchase. I didn't just squirrel it away for a rainy day. And I didn't follow the standard advice to pay it off my horrible credit card debt. No, I *managed* it in exactly the same way I did with every other penny that came my way by putting 10% in each of my various accounts.

And so more little things began to happen. A joint venture partner presented me with a $3000 payment for a deal I had forgotten all about. But there were also smaller financial miracles: my car repairs were far less than usual. I would go shopping and find all my usual brands at half price. I got a nice tax rebate. The council told me I had massively overpaid my council tax, years ago, when I was just a student. The overpayment was thousands and the council just sent me a cheque in the post.

These sorts of things became more commonplace. My books began selling far better without any additional marketing. Books that had languished in the pit of obscurity started climbing the sales charts, with no explanation. These financial miracles began to increase, and increase in frequency until it became impossible to explain them as coincidence even if I had tried.

And then the snowball effect really kicked in. It seemed the less I needed money, the more it came to me.

I remember the first time I realised I was about to go over the VAT threshold. In the UK, any business with a turnover greater than a certain amount must register for VAT. As it was nearing the end of the year and I really couldn't face the headache and extra administration involved in registering for VAT, I decided to stop working, releasing no new books, and to 'coast' for the last few months, in an attempt to stay under the VAT threshold until next year.

That very month I had my biggest *ever* month. The next month of the year was even greater. Without doing any work at all, I managed to manifest a truly enormous sum of money, rocketing me above the VAT threshold.

(The really funny thing was that when I sat down with my accountant, he told me I had misunderstood the tax rules anyway, so I *still* wouldn't have to register. Talk about a silver lining!)

It's obvious why this happened. I didn't need money to the extent that I was happy to earn *less,* rather than to risk having extra work. And so, because I was not grasping, not asking, not even needing more money…

…the universe just gave me loads more.

And so I learned first hand the real reason why the rich get richer and the poor get poorer. The richer you feel, think and act – the richer you get.

16 How to Live on 60%

But this means living on less than I do currently. Save 40%? – Not a chance! I am barely able to make ends meet now.

I can fully appreciate that many of you will only be able to save the minimum of 1% into each account every month.

But before you decide to do that, stop and think for a moment: could you *possibly* save the full 40% (10% into each account) and still cover your day-to-day living? Could you do it for one month? If your work hours were suddenly cut by 40%, could you survive for a month? If your life depended on it, could you do it?

Make no mistake. That first month will be hard. I am talking about some serious economising here. I am talking about making cheap meals at home with a lot of pasta and potatoes. I am talking of not buying newspapers, magazines or *any* non-essentials. I am talking of shopping in the cheap supermarket. I am talking of buying the plain-branded value items. No coffees from cafés. No petrol in the car or bus tickets if you can walk instead. Buy budget washing powder. Make coffee at home. Buy cheap vegetables and cook from scratch. If you smoke, cut it down by 50%. If you drink, cut half of that out too. Could you do this, just for a month or two?

When I started out, I had *huge* outgoings and very little income. But somehow, I still managed to put away the full 40% each month, even while working for minimum wage. I found I was able to live on a fraction of what I had previously done.

How did I do it? I became an expert at cheap and healthy eating. I walked whenever I could rather than taking the car. I visited friends and had them come to me, rather than paying for expensive social occasions. If I did find myself in a pub, I drank orange squash rather than expensive wine, telling people I was on a health kick. I cancelled my gym membership and started walking everywhere. I cancelled my subscriptions to all non-essential services. I annoyed my credit card companies by swapping back and forth between 0% deals to get my repayments down. And I paid *everything* on monthly direct debit. (This is helpful for disorganised people to avoid danger of frequent large bills.) Another way to effortlessly spend less is to commit to using cash rather than credit or debit cards for all purchases (other than direct debit bills). By seeing that cash leave your purse or wallet every time you spend, you will unconsciously end up with a far greater awareness of the amount you spend on everyday items and will automatically begin economising.

'But isn't all this economising going to make me feel MORE like a pauper?'

To a certain extent, this is true. But self-imposed austerity isn't even remotely as destructive as unbridled, out of control poverty and desperation. Remember, you aren't being forced to eat cheap meat through poverty, you are *choosing* to eat cheap meat and put the excess money to better use.

I really came to enjoy separating my money into different accounts. I loved seeing the balances grow. I even came to view each little economy as a step towards greater riches. And so, rather than feeling poor, I found the whole process actually made me feel richer and more in control right from the beginning.

I knew it wouldn't be forever. I knew it was all building towards a better life. So it became a bit of a game. I came to enjoy being frugal, finding more creative and better ways of saving money. Because this austerity was self-imposed, it didn't feel like hardship. I was in control of this. It was something *I* was doing, a goal I was working towards. I was not living in poverty; I was doing *Magic!*

I came to view the actual moving of the money as a kind of ritual, a Magical spell. I felt that every time I managed money, I became that little bit richer and so found the whole process thoroughly enjoyable. And it gave me such a buzz to see the account balances increasing and the debts decreasing – *a far greater buzz than frivolous spending ever did.*

If you really, *really* aren't able to put away 10% into each account and so live on 60% of your income (and many of you won't be), start with just 5%. If you can't afford 5%, just do 1%.

But always do it.

Increase the percentages as slowly as you like, but the faster you can get to 10% in each separate account, the faster things will change for you financially. And the faster things change, the shorter the time you must spend doing this tough economising. The long-term payoff from this short-term austerity really is enormous.

In my experience, when people put away the full 40% (10% into each account), it only takes around 3-4 months to start the Magic working. Sometimes, the effect is almost instantaneous.

17 Remember to Spend your Fun Money

This system is *not* just all about saving; it's also about spending. It may sound like an obvious point, but please make sure you actually *spend* your Fun money.

I was so unused to spending money on myself that the Fun account caused me to be very uncomfortable in the beginning. I think I had actually forgotten how to have fun with money. In the early days I had to force myself to spend this money on myself. I didn't even enjoy it. It felt irresponsible. After all, how on earth could I waste money on fun and frivolity when I had £30k owing on credit cards?

I would dither and fuss and end up letting the account grow fuller and fuller until it became hundreds. The fuller the account became, the harder it was for me to contemplate frittering it away on myself. I would then end up spending it on essentials, or telling myself that 'paying off my credit card was a luxury'.

Big mistake. Spending money on yourself is not a secondary option. It is not something to be done once all the other bills are paid. Spending money on yourself is an essential part of the whole process. Until you can learn to spend money on *you*, you will never feel truly rich. And as we know, until you can feel truly rich, you will not attract riches.

The Fun account is created to give you the experience of treating yourself – of spending on fun, frivolous or luxury purchases, not randomly or indiscriminately, but within set limits, *just like a rich person does*. Some other writers recommend spending *all* the money in this account every month but I find that zeroing my Fun account leaves me feeling poor again. I would always leave a buffer of around £50-100, just so that I didn't ever see that account empty.

When spending Fun money, the idea is to spend money on things you *want*, not just on things you *need*. This money should make you feel spoiled, pampered and rich. So don't ever choose the cheaper option simply because it's better value. Doing this goes against the whole point of Fun money. For example, if you fancy buying a new pair of jeans, don't go to the cheap store because you can buy two pairs that you don't really like. Go to the store you really love and buy one pair that you can be proud of. Enjoy the attention in the changing rooms, and the quality of the paper bag they are placed in. Spending Fun money should make you feel rich and treated. Of course, if you *prefer* the jeans in the value store, buy them. But don't ever choose the cheaper option *just because it's cheaper*, not when spending Fun money, anyway.

If you go out for a nice meal with your Fun money (something I love to do), avoid looking for the cheapest thing on the menu. In the early days, don't go for the fillet steak if you feel uncomfortable paying for such an expensive dish. But do try just going up to the second or third cheapest, rather than automatically picking the cheapest meal on the menu. Even now, I have to resist the temptation to choose the absolute cheapest meal on the menu. This was a habit of mine for so long that it's hard to shake off. I still feel a naughty thrill when I choose a bottle of wine from the bottom of the list rather than the house wine. Perhaps I always will…

So give up all feelings of guilt in spending your Fun money, even if you have children. Remember, the universe doesn't allocate money according to deserve or need. It allocates money according to the person you are. And if your persona radiates 'everyone is more important than me' then that's what the universe reflects back at you.

Fun money is as essential as any other account. And don't try and kid yourself that paying off a credit card or buying something for the children is a 'luxury'. It's not.

'But that's irresponsible. My children must come first and my daughter is desperate for a new winter coat.'

I am not telling you that it is forbidden to spend your Fun money on your children. Your priorities are your business and financial decisions are yours and yours alone. I am just saying that every time you spend Fun money on something 'more important' than yourself, you prolong and reinforce the current situation. While you place yourself and your own needs at the bottom of a huge pile that includes your children, credit cards, utility companies and the government, the universe will continue to send you the scraps. While you have this little respect for your own personal need for fun and fulfilment, while you see yourself as less important than everyone else in your life, the universe isn't going to view you as important either.

Remember, we are only talking about a little percentage of your weekly or monthly money here –10% *at most.* Are you not worth even 10% of your own hard-earned cash? Of course you are! And believe me, by spending this on yourself, you are moving closer and closer to the situation where your children will never want for anything.

18 Emergency! I Need to Raid the Accounts

If you currently have severe money troubles then the chances are that at some point after starting money managing, you will find yourself in the following difficult position.

You need to raid the accounts.

This happens to almost everyone, so don't feel bad if you find yourself in this situation. Some expense has come in, or you may simply need to buy food, and your current account is empty. But you *do* have a nice little stash in your Fun account and your Big Purchase account.

So what *should* you do?

First of all, is there *any* way you can avoid raiding the accounts?

This happened to me many times in the first year of working with Magic when I would inevitably raid my other accounts to pay for unexpected bills. Usually, the Fun account would be first for the chop, followed by the Big Purchase money.

I am sure that my situation would have improved more quickly had I stuck better to the plan in the early days, and not raided the accounts month after month. Because it was only when I made the firm decision not to raid my accounts under any circumstances (to fully control my money rather than be controlled *by* money) that things really began to pick up.

It took about seven months for me to completely turn my finances around whereas my partner, as I said previously, saw an immediate and dramatic upturn almost the moment he started managing his money. It's interesting that he never once raided his accounts for any reason. He always felt this would 'break the Magic', and I now tend to agree with him.

I most categorically and emphatically am *not* advising anyone to leave any particular bill outstanding, nor to allow their overdraft to go into the red!

All I am trying to do is to get you to see the importance of avoiding raiding *whenever possible.* Dipping into the accounts once or twice in emergencies probably isn't going to cause much damage. But if you persist in raiding the accounts every month, it won't be long before your fortunes turn sour again.

Raiding won't bring immediate disaster, but it does slow down all the good you have been doing with your money management. Of course, there is an immediate short-term payoff to raiding accounts – resolution and relieving of your current financial emergency. But longer term, the effect is to put a halt to the financial security that is coming your way. Before long, you will find yourself back at square one without a penny in any of your accounts. You can either take my word for it, or you can find out for yourself, but raiding accounts just works to set you back.

So if you are thinking of raiding one of the accounts, this is the question you need to ask yourself: is raiding this account worth 'breaking the Magic' for?

Sometimes the answer will be yes.

But by asking this question each time you are tempted you will often find you can avoid raiding and stay on track. If you do need to raid an account, do your utmost to return to your money management immediately. Don't assume you've 'blown it' for this month and let everything go. The longer you stay on track, the easier and more effective it all becomes.

If raiding is happening frequently and inescapably, go down to putting just 5% or 2% or 1% into each account. The Magic will still work with a lower percentage; it will just mean that financial security may come more slowly for you.

If you find yourself needing to raid accounts every month, consider making your fourth account an Emergency Bills account.

It was this constant need to raid my other accounts that led to my setting up an additional 'Emergency

Bills' account. By setting up the emergency bills account, I was able to overcome my continual raiding of the other accounts. I also achieved incredible peace of mind and a feeling of safety from knowing this fund was acting as a buffer to protect me from disasters such as financial snap-backs. This peace of mind alone had a hugely beneficial effect on my finances.

19 Victory Over the Snap-Back

There is a wonderful additional benefit to money-managing – it helps to protect you from that horror of all horrors – the financial snap-back.

As previously mentioned, this is the horrifying experience of having things go suddenly and drastically wrong, *just as you thought you had turned a corner.* The snap-back tends to happen when a fantastic, life-changing manifestation occurs. You may have apparently manifested a huge sum of money.

But then… it all comes crashing down. A huge and unexpected bill wipes out all your new-found money.

I think this happens for the following reason. If you are not *ready* to receive the manifestation, *it won't stick around!* If you have worked a piece of Magic but have not worked sufficiently on *you*, on turning yourself into a person that *fits* that goal, *then you will lose it.*

I am naturally a scatterbrain. I have *no* natural organisational skills at all. And before I started this plan, I was always terrible at organising my money. I can remember so many times when I was in my twenties when I would sit with a huge stack of bills, working out what I could pay to each company. I would often have to phone each one, and beg for a little extra time or an instalment plan. To this day, my filing system consists of several piles of paperwork (often going back years). My computer desktop has approximately one hundred icons because I have no computer folder system. Little wonder that money kept leaving me in increasingly violent snap-backs. Think like a financial scatterbrain and your money will scatter.

I have always been this way and most of the time I don't seek to change it. Generally speaking, too much organisation and strict rules make me feel uncomfortable. But when it comes to my finances, it is now a very different story. Scatterbrains like me need something in place to ensure that their financial situation isn't equally disorganised. Never in my life had I saved money in a tax account, even during long periods of self-employment. And because of this, I lived in constant fear of receiving my next tax bill.

After starting money management, instantly, that fear was gone. Managing my money was a total revelation to me. It was like an enormous, insurmountable and constant weight had suddenly been lifted from my shoulders. The Emergency Bill account alone was enough to give me an immeasurable feeling of security. And to this day, I still put a percentage of my income into my tax account every month. And because of this, I never, ever, have any worries about paying my tax bill.

Successful and committed money management works extremely well to help you avoid these horrible snap-backs: because you behave in a sensible, organised, *rich* way when you do receive money, the universe isn't so quick to snatch it back off you again.

Snap-back avoided!

20 Let's Go Back to the Nitty Gritty

Let's go back to the plan because I'm sure by now you have a lot of questions about the details. Let me show you *exactly* how I would manage my money in the early days.

Let's manage £1300 of employed take-home (after tax) salary or business dividends. £1300 was my take-home wage at the factory when I started this plan.

10% For local charitable cause   = £130

10% Fun money   = £130

10% Big Purchase   = £130

10% Emergency Bills   = £130

Leaving   = £780 for living

When things began to pick up for me financially and my income increased, there were fewer occasions when I became out of control with my bills. The result was that the Emergency Bills account started to grow and grow. Once I had a buffer of several thousand pounds, it seemed pointless to continue putting so much into this account.

At this point, I switched from putting money into an Emergency Bills account to paying that 10% every month toward my credit card debt over and above my normal monthly repayments. Paying off my debts made me feel fabulous even when it was just a tiny amount. Because I knew that my monthly outgoings decreased each time I paid off a bit of credit card debt, I felt a little richer every time I did it.

Once my debts were gone, I finally set up my Golden Goose account. Remember, the purpose of this account is not to make purchases but to invest in things that will grow and secure your future by giving you a passive income – for me this investment was property.

And of course, while I still separate every penny that comes to me, these days I give a good deal more than 10% to charity.

It isn't in any way essential that you do exactly as I did. The rules are *not* fixed. You may decide to jiggle the percentages – perhaps putting 5% in one account and 10% in another. You might even decide to have a different account, perhaps one I haven't mentioned.

I don't generally recommend you have more than four accounts in addition to your normal checking or current account. Otherwise things can get a little too unwieldy and difficult. The only exception to this is if you are self-employed. If you haven't already done so, every self-employed person *must* have a separate tax account with which to pay tax bills at the end of the year. Your accountant will have a good idea of a suitable percentage.

The important thing is to designate your accounts for just those purposes that are meaningful to you. *Please don't* write to me to ask me to look over your particular plan and tell you that it's okay. I cannot advise in very specific circumstances. This is not because I don't have the time, or that I can't be bothered; it is because only you will know the answer to your question through your own intuition about what 'feels' right and from experiencing your particular plan in action.

Questions such as:

Is it okay if I give to my own relative?

Is it okay to put 10% into Emergency Bills and 5% into Fun?

Can I combine two of these accounts and make my own special account for a particular purpose?

I would love a fifth account and I am sure I can manage it, is this okay?

Can I pay for a holiday/car using half Fun money and Big Purchase money?

don't matter!

All that matters is that you are saving, spending and giving money away in measured and manageable amounts.

So the answer to any of these sorts of questions is to try it and see how it makes you feel. If you feel sorted, in control, confident, relaxed about any 'tweak' you want to make, it probably will work better than sticking rigidly to the plan as laid out, or than following any specific instruction I may give you. If any change to the plan feels like you are 'breaking the Magic', it is likely to do exactly that.

If you really don't know where to start and prefer just to follow a set plan, I recommend you just do as I did: i.e. set aside an amount for tax (if you are self-employed) and then have the standard four accounts as described.

1. Big Purchase Account

2. Fun account

3. Giving to others account

4. Emergency Bills account

21 Giving to Others and Money Management:
The Two Steps to the Magical Receiving State

Let's recall and reiterate some key points:

Manifesting a lot of money:

while being resentful of those who have it;

while thinking having money is your 'right' or that society 'owes' it to you;

while being controlled by it/afraid of it;

while thinking money makes you selfish;

while feeling constantly needy, wanting and desperate for it;

while thinking it is too materialistic or beneath you;

while thinking you are undeserving of wealth;

while being constantly terrified of losing it

is almost impossible.

Every time you say 'I can't afford it', *you won't afford it.*

Every time you mismanage your money, you tell the universe that you are not capable of handling more.

Every time you think or say *I'm not one of the rich ones*, you are not one of the rich ones.

Every time you have feelings of anger, resentment or confusion over money, you place yourself in the class of have-nots.

Why?

Because all of these things keep you out of the Magical receiving state.

All of these negative feelings and actions are evidence of your *desperately wanting things to be different*. These things are evidence that you are stuck in *wanting and asking* and hence not *receiving*. They show just how far you are from the state of trust and non-wanting that is the signature of the Magical receiving state.

By making the two very *practical* moves of:

a) Giving to others and

b) Managing your money,

you will find yourself naturally closer to the Magical receiving state. You will find changing any negative feelings easy and even automatic. You will begin to feel the sort of 'respectful neutrality' toward money that comes when it no longer rules your life.

Giving to others and *managing your money* are really just tools for getting you into the Magical receiving state that allows everything you want to flow into your life.

22 Charging Things Up: Telling a New Story

After a few months of money-managing, you will feel more in control of your money and things will be financially easier. It is important that this financial upturn is reflected in the way you conduct the rest of your life.

You need to begin *being* the person you want to be. And one of the most important ways in which you can ensure that your everyday being reflects the new financially comfortable *you*, is by attending to your language and the story you tell.

One of the simplest and most effective ways to bring something into your life is just to start telling the story that you already have that thing, or that it is coming to you. As you become richer, your story is going to have to change anyway. So why not start telling that positive story *now,* and power-up your progress to becoming rich? This does not necessarily mean repeating affirmations such as 'I have a million dollars', because as you may have discovered, that sort of cast-iron statement is too easy for your mind to counter with a *'no you don't; you're overdrawn at the bank'.*

I love affirmations, but I find they work far, far better if you start small and move up in intensity. If you are barely surviving, your saying 'I am a millionaire' may sound very nice, but you can repeat that statement for the next twenty years and nothing would really happen. But by starting with a lesser, more believable statement, the affirmation has a really good chance of taking hold immediately.

I'm talking about thinking and saying things such as 'I feel a lot less worried about money now; money seems to be flowing to me; I feel so much richer these days; I am becoming one of the rich ones; my money troubles seem to be lessening.' These are all things that are much harder for your mind to argue with than 'I have a million dollars'.

And I'm not just talking about formal affirmations; the way you speak to others, your partner, your parents, your friends, and in your own internal monologue – these have a far greater effect on you than the odd positive affirmation.

If you have always struggled for money, it is very likely that you have been telling a story of poverty, lack, want and possibly injustice for your entire life. Your parents may well have told this story while you were small. And so you were brought up with a feeling of lack, scarcity or unworthiness.

If you are saying 'I wish I had more money' or 'I can't afford it' several times a day, look no further for reasons for your money troubles. This little phrase *I can't afford it* becomes like a constant affirmation of your financial situation, keeping you stuck down in the realms of the people who never make it financially.

Remember: every statement of 'I can't afford it' just reinforces your state of poverty, 'denting' the Magic and putting a halt on all the good that could be coming your way. So, instead of saying 'I can't afford it', try saying 'I haven't set enough money aside for that yet', or 'that can wait for next month'.

Out of reach purchases are not things you 'can't afford' they are merely things you 'haven't budgeted for this month'. Or they are things to be bought with your Big Purchase money only *when* the balance in that account is high enough.

The effect of telling this sort of story is subtle, but very, very effective. It works to slowly but surely change your beliefs.

The things you do, think and say, both to others and privately to yourself, are inspired by your beliefs. But things you say also work to *reinforce* those beliefs. It's like a feedback loop.

This means that rather than waiting for the belief to change to start speaking like a rich person, you can effectively start speaking like a rich person first and then eventually the belief will follow. And when your belief is that you are rich, you will naturally begin to speak, think and act like a rich person without any conscious effort.

When you have been managing your money for a few months, there will be money in your accounts. Take the time just to log in to your online banking and gloat over your accounts, or count all the cash in your piggy banks. There may be only a few pounds or dollars in each, but it's still more than you would have had before starting managing. Take every opportunity to bask in what money you do have.

When the money started to flood in for me, I found it hugely empowering to sit with my partner and talk about money. It went from being a source of tension and anxiety to being one of our main topics of conversation. I went from saying 'I can't afford it' to reporting 'I'm the richest person I know'.

Of course, this sounds horribly distasteful and I would never do it publicly. But please understand… this boasting was not gloating or competitiveness. I was not seeking to put others down in order to place myself above them. This 'boasting' was done consciously in order to eradicate and cancel out the effect of 40 years of thinking that everyone around me had more money than I did. It was an intentional act of placing myself amongst the 'haves' rather than negatively labelling myself as one of the 'have nots'. It felt quite odd and almost uncomfortable at first, but it soon began to feel more normal to speak of myself as one of the rich ones.

23 Charging Things Up:
Helping the Universe Along

This book is concerned with what I am calling Magic – the ability to attract things into your life. But you will certainly hurry things up by taking physical action too.

Even if you follow all the instructions so far, the universe is very unlikely to offer you a lottery win, a surprise inheritance or a chest of treasure in the bottom of your garden. It is *very* likely to offer you opportunities that will lead to your receiving gradually bigger and bigger sums of money. But it's far harder to see these opportunities in the first place unless you are busy, active, and meeting new people. Yes, you could just sit on your sofa waiting for money to fall out of the sky, or you could give the universe a helping hand and take physical steps in the direction of becoming rich.

My hairdresser recently told me a joke that is very fitting here.

One day there is a huge and terrible flood, covering the land in water. In one little village the flood is particularly bad. But the local priest isn't afraid. After all, he believes that God would never let him drown and will certainly come to save him. So he sits on his roof and prays hard, waiting for God to save him. Presently, a boat comes by with a friendly stranger aboard. 'Hop on,' says the stranger. 'I'll take you to safety!'

'No, it's okay, you go on,' says our priest. 'God will save me'. So he prays a bit harder and the water rises higher. Soon another boat comes by. 'Come aboard,' says the driver. 'I'll take you to safety.'

'No thanks. You go on. God will save me,' says our minister. So he prays a bit harder and sits and waits for God to save him. The water rises further until it is up to his neck. At the last moment, another boat comes along. 'Quickly, get in!' calls the boatman. 'I'll take you to safety!'

'No, no! You go on, I know God will save me,' he says as the water reaches his chin. The water rises over his head and he drowns.

On reaching heaven, our man asks for an audience with God. He asks him 'Lord, I prayed and prayed, I asked and asked for help. Why didn't you save me?'

'What do you mean?' says God, 'I sent you three boats!'

I like to take the following moral from this story: if you sit on your backside all day, watching television, playing computer games, waiting for the lottery win, you probably won't even *notice* the opportunities that the universe is trying desperately to present to you.

So *do things.*

Don't be lazy with your Magic. If you are employed, look for promotion. If you have no chance of promotion, look for a new job. If you love your badly-paying job, try to set up a little business in your spare time. What are you interested in? Start a blog and sell advertising space. Sell jewellery, write a book, make cakes, fix computers, buy and sell clothes on eBay. Learn about Forex or be on the lookout for investment opportunities, especially if you have a Golden Goose account. If you have no education, get some. Go to evening classes or take a training course. If you are unemployed, look for a job or do some free government training. Volunteer. Join a club. Go for a walk.

Do stuff.

It doesn't really matter what these first moves are as these will likely only be stepping-stones to greater things. Do *anything* as long as it is in the direction of something new or different. Keep your eyes open and when good opportunities are offered to you, *take them.* You never know where a particular move will take you. You don't have to find a million-pound business idea off the bat. What is important is that you are taking new steps, making new moves, opening new opportunities, meeting new people.

Don't wait for change, *be* the change.

A few years ago, while working on my first book, I used to meet another writer occasionally in a café where I liked to write. He was working on a memoir of his extraordinary early life. We were both quite green at the time and both had great fear and excitement at the thought of releasing our first books. That was around six years ago.

Just recently, I met this man again. 'How's the book coming along,' he asked. I looked puzzled at him. 'Which one?' I replied. We chatted for a few minutes; just long enough for me to find out he was still working on that same first book.

'Just publish it!' I told him. 'The first is the hardest. Take that first step. You'll be glad you did!'

'Yes, perhaps,' he replied. 'But I've read on the Internet that it's a bad idea to release a book in the summer, so maybe I'll look at doing it in the autumn.'

I wonder where he might have been now if only he had published six years ago.

In my own case, I didn't sit down one day to write a bestselling book. I started out by learning the basics of web design, with the intention of selling educational materials online. *This business was a complete and utter disaster*. But I didn't despair at my apparent failure because I had begun experimenting with Magic at this point. *I trusted and looked for the silver lining. This was just a stepping-*

stone. After all, this failed business certainly led to my knowing more about the Internet and how it works. I continued to manage my money, and continued to look for opportunity.

My first fumbling attempt at writing was an e-book, written on my days off, and sold directly from an ugly, clumsy, self-built website. Again, my sales were pitiful. *But I trusted. I felt the Magic. I noticed the roses. This was just another stepping-stone.* After all, I had written a book and that was a triumph in itself, I just hadn't found the right platform on which to sell it. So I shifted from websites to other forms of publishing. I honed my writing skills and this led to my first paperback book. Then came Kindle, audiobooks and finally my other business ventures. I have now written many, many books and have three websites. But none of this would have happened without that first, part-time, floundering dabble into Internet marketing. And the truth is, even after all these years, I never *have* had much success in Internet marketing! Internet marketing remains a 'failure' for me, in the traditional sense. But this expensive failure turned out to be *the* essential stepping-stone to my becoming hugely successful in a completely different area. I never set out with any plan become a writer, let alone a bestselling author. Yet somehow, that is what I have become.

I only became successful when I discovered Magic. But this discovery did not mean I just stopped working and sat on my bottom waiting for things to fall into my lap. I have worked hard my whole life and I still work just as hard. It's just that now I only work doing things I love, and everything I work at has an enchanted feel to it.

Yes, I have used *Magic* to manifest an exceptional life. I have stopped almost *all* complaining. I have manifested for others. I have let go and trusted. I have diligently managed all the money that has come to me into separate accounts. I started telling a new story of wealth. I stayed in the delicious receiving state for longer and longer periods of time.

But that's not *all* I have done. I have taken a lot of action too. I have taken risks and made mistakes. I have never stopped moving in the direction of better things.

As I began to master Magic, my writing began to feel like the words were enchanted. It became easy, and my books became so successful that it seemed everything I wrote turned to gold.

But I still had to write the books in the first place!

If I had continued to sit around in poverty, shouting at the television, waiting for the lottery win, repeating affirmations and wondering my vision board wasn't working, I would probably still be sitting there now.

24 A Quick Recipe for Money Magic

Let me give you a shorthand version of the perfect recipe for making Magical money. I have used exactly this formula many times with great success.

1. *Prepare* by taking complete responsibility for sorting out your financial situation. Make this easier by keeping a gratitude journal and going on a 'negativity fast'. For more help read *A Complaint Free Life* by Will Bowen

2. Decide that your manifestation will be at least partly for someone else.

3. Begin managing your money immediately.

4. *Trust in the process* and don't keep wondering when your manifestation is coming. *If* you ask the universe for money, *don't ask again.*

5. Tell a new story of riches. If things don't appear to be going your way, always look for a silver lining. See all apparent misfortune as a stepping-stone to greater things

6. Keep active and keep your eyes open for opportunity

7. When money begins to come in greater amounts, continue to manage diligently.

That's it. There is no one quick trick, no one secret thing. But this is what I have done over and over and is what I continue to do to this day.

It works so well it's almost unfair.

25 What's to Come?
The Future is Bright

At some point, you will reach the tipping point when suddenly everything gets much, much easier. The austerity measures will lessen and eventually stop.

And then, it will all have been worth it. All those difficult months, all that scrimping and saving will have paid off. The money managing has become habit. The accounts are full. You no longer have to contrive to think rich thoughts or say rich things. You will automatically find yourself feeling richer, speaking richer and acting richer.

Things will still be up and down. Sometimes you will lose a bit; sometimes an unexpected expense will come along. But with this plan in place, these normal ups and downs no longer have the power to unsettle you. There are no more financial disasters. There are no more snap-backs. Any financial 'misfortune' will be easily and automatically dismissed as a stepping-stone to something greater and more wonderful. You will begin to feel immune to financial ruin.

Magically speaking, you will be in such a different place to where you are now. Ironically, it is when you are in this state that the big money is likely to begin to roll in. When you no longer *want* for money, it will be everywhere and people will fall over themselves to give it to you. You will feel sorted, organised, in control. You will have a completely different attitude to wealth, money and rich people. You will no longer resent people with a lot of money. You will come to see that most of them are ordinary people just like you, just with different attitudes and actions towards money. You will move from resenting the rich to pitying those who do so. If you are a kind, caring person now, nothing will change when you get money. You will just be able to genuinely help those people you care so much about. And when you can easily and regularly change the lives of those you love or care deeply about, be they friends and family or needy strangers, you will experience true happiness, purpose and belonging.

You will have shifted into a calmer, less resentful, more grateful and less needy place. This will have a knock-on effect on everything else in your life. When money starts to come tumbling your way in a manner that goes far beyond mere coincidence, you will no longer doubt that Magic exists.

You will become more powerful than you knew was possible. Without the monstrous confusion and headache of financial worry, you will be free to do what you want with life. And only *then* will the real fun start, not because you suddenly can buy lots pretty things and shiny gadgets, but because of where money can take you, because of what it frees up. Designer handbags and Gucci shoes, mere trinkets and ostentation are *nothing* compared to the greater riches in store. Now you have the time and resources to work out what truly makes you happy. Freedom, the world, the oyster has opened before you.

Now go out and play!

How to Enter the Charity Draw

To be in with a chance of your chosen charity receiving a donation from me, simply visit this webpage and add your email to the list.

http://eepurl.com/btpTmD

Approximately twice yearly I will pick one name at random from the list and contact them personally to ask for their chosen charity. The charity of your choice can be large or small, and in any country. But it must be a **registered charity** and be able to accept payment by bank transfer or Paypal.

No purchase is necessary. Anyone may enter.

The list to which you will subscribe is 100% private and accessed by me and only me. I never spam with third-party products and wouldn't *dream* of passing your details on to anyone else. Your email will remain on the list for as long as I continue to run the charity draw. You may of course unsubscribe at any time.

I will take $1 for every book sold or borrowed and add it to the fund. If I sell 100 books, I will give away \$100. If I sell 1000 books, I will give away \$1000. If I sell 10,000 books… you get the point. So I ask you to share this book with others, to tell your Facebook friends, your Twitter contacts. The more people buy, the bigger each charity donation will be.

Just to add to the Magic, the first draw will take place on 21st December – the Magical winter solstice. The next draw will be 21st June, the summer solstice. Thus twice yearly, one of my lovely readers will enjoy a very nice summer or Christmas surprise.

Blessings,
Genny Davis

Further Reading

Books on Magic by Genevieve Davis

Becoming Magic
Doing Magic
Advanced Magic

Books on Money Managing

T. Harv Eker, *Secrets of the Millionaire Mind*
George S Clason, *The Richest Man in Babylon*

On Kicking Complaining

Will Bowen, *A Complaint Free World*

Other books that have influenced or had a big impact on me

Eckhart Tolle, *The Power of Now*
Eckhart Tolle, *A New Earth*
Esther Hicks, *The Astonishing Power of Emotions*
Wayne Dyer, *The Power of Intention*

Printed in Great Britain
by Amazon